THE
OFFICIAL
BEGINNER'S GUIDE FOR
ACT

THE
OFFICIAL
BEGINNER'S GUIDE FOR
ACT

ACT

WILEY

Contents

Introduction vii

Chapter 1: Overview and Purpose of PreACT® Diagnostic 1
Your PreACT Diagnostic Results... 3
Your PreACT Diagnostic Score Report 5
What Do Your Scores Mean? 5
Your Predicted ACT Score Ranges... 6
Your Detailed Results... 6
Building Your Skills 7

Chapter 2: About the ACT 9
Description of the Full ACT Test 10
English Test.. 10
Mathematics Test... 12
Reading Test 20
Science Test 23
Writing Test (Optional).. 25
The Fifth Test and Section Retesting 27
ACT Test Formats: Paper and Online.. 27
Using a Calculator 27
Taking the Test 28
Notes... 30

Chapter 3: Taking a Practice Test 31
Simulating Testing Conditions 32
Practice Test 37

Chapter 4: Scoring Your Practice Test 95
Scoring Your Practice Test 96
Scoring Your Multiple-Choice Tests 97
Scoring Your Practice Writing Test Essay.. 103

Chapter 5: Interpreting Your ACT Test Scores and Ranks 109
Understanding Your ACT Test Results... 111
How ACT Scores Your Multiple-Choice Tests 111
How ACT Scores Your Writing Test.. 111
Recognizing That Test Scores Are Estimates of Educational Achievement........... 111
Using Ranks to Interpret Your Scores.. 112
Comparing Your Test Scores to Each Other 112

Comparing Your Scores and Ranks to Your High School Grades 112

Comparing Your Scores to Those of Enrolled First-Year College Students 112

Using ACT College and Career Readiness Standards to Help You Understand
    Your ACT Scores 113

Planning Your Education and Career... 114

Seeking Additional Information and Guidance... 114

ACT College and Career Readiness Standards—English 115

    Production of Writing... 115

ACT College and Career Readiness Standards—Mathematics...................... 122

ACT College and Career Readiness Standards—Reading 131

    Text Complexity Rubric—Reading 138

ACT College and Career Readiness Standards—Science.............................. 145

Introduction

The ACT is your gateway to some of the world's best colleges and universities. These schools use your ACT score to evaluate your application and determine your eligibility for a scholarship. Imagine how graduation from a top university will help you achieve success in both career and life.

Fortunately, achieving a high score, and thus being accepted—and perhaps even earning a scholarship—to a good school, is within your reach. It's not just a matter of natural skill; it's a matter of practice and guidance. Each topic on the exam is covered in high school, so nothing on the ACT is new. If you see an ACT question on a new topic, you'll probably see that topic in class before the year is over.

The plan is simple. Start with the online PreACT Diagnostic, which you can find at www .preactdiagnostic.com/guidebook. Check your scores with the guide in this book on page 5, and this will show you some of your strengths along with areas that need practice. Next, take the ACT practice test on page 37 so you can go through the experience of taking the actual exam. This practice enables you to make mistakes on a trial test, not on the real thing. Check and review your answers and note the topics and skills where you need practice. Mark the questions you missed from simple blunders, such as misreading the question, making mistakes with simple math, or running out of steam.

If you need help, you're not alone. Most students who score well had lots of practice, and you can also practice and do well. Also, no one gets a perfect score, so you shouldn't expect to. You just need to score well enough to be a competitive applicant to your target school. (Check the university's admission requirements for the ACT score that is considered competitive or talk with your school counselor.)

Your ACT score is just one of many parts of your college application. Schools also look at your GPA, work experience, volunteer experience, sports, school activities, student government, and even hobbies. Schools like to see a candidate who can bring diverse skills and experiences to the university culture—but even among your strengths, your ACT score can make or break the deal. Your path to success begins right here, right now, on the next page.

Chapter 1:
Overview and Purpose of PreACT® Diagnostic

PreACT Diagnostic is an online version of the PreACT® and is designed to provide a practice experience for students planning to take the ACT. PreACT Diagnostic provides Composite, subject, and STEM scores, along with predicted ACT score ranges, and helps students to identify areas of strength and weakness for further preparation for the ACT.

PreACT Diagnostic is a multiple-choice test that covers all four ACT subject areas (English, math, reading, and science) with a slightly shorter test time (2 hours, 10 minutes versus 2 hours, 55 minutes for the ACT). PreACT Diagnostic does not include a writing component. Table 1.1 provides a description of the four PreACT Diagnostic test sections.

Table 1.1: PreACT Diagnostic Test Sections

Section	Content Description	Format
English questions: 45 **Time allotted:** 30 minutes	Measures a student's understanding of the conventions of standard written English, production of writing, and knowledge of language	Three essays, or passages, each accompanied by a sequence of multiple-choice test questions
Math questions: 36 **Time allotted:** 40 minutes	Measures skills students have typically acquired in high school math courses and emphasizes major content areas that are prerequisites to successful performance in entry-level courses in college mathematics: • Requires use of quantitative reasoning skills to solve practical problems • Requires demonstrating some computational skills and recall of basic formulas Students may use a calculator for the math test as outlined in the ACT calculator policy. The overall math score is used along with the science score to compute the STEM score.	36 independent multiple-choice questions, with some questions sharing the same information
Reading questions: 25 **Time allotted:** 30 minutes	Measures the student's reading comprehension The questions ask students to derive meaning from the reading passages. Specifically, the questions ask students to do the following: • Use referring and reasoning skills to determine main ideas • Locate and interpret significant details • Understand sequences of events • Make comparisons • Comprehend cause-effect relationships • Determine the meaning of context-dependent words, phrases, and statements	Three essays, or passages, each accompanied by a number of multiple-choice test questions

Section	Content Description	Format
	• Draw generalizations • Analyze the author's or narrator's voice and method. The test includes a mix of literary narrative and informational passages that are representative of the levels and kinds of text commonly encountered in the 11th and 12th grade and first-year college curricula.	
Science questions: 30 **Time allotted:** 30 minutes	Measures scientific reasoning skills acquired in general introductory courses in the natural sciences This test is based on the type of content typically covered in early high school science courses.	Five sets of scientific information, each followed by a number of multiple-choice test questions

Within each section, PreACT Diagnostic covers the same reporting categories as those covered in the ACT.

PreACT Diagnostic is aligned to the same 1–36 ACT Score Scale. PreACT Diagnostic is a shorter and slightly less difficult test than the ACT, therefore the highest possible score is 35.

PreACT Diagnostic does not collect information regarding high school course work, student interests, or career plans.

By taking the PreACT Diagnostic, you will

- Gain exposure to the types of questions and content featured on the ACT test

- Gain exposure to the testing experience of taking the ACT test

- Gain a prediction of how you are likely to perform on the ACT test

- Gain an understanding of your strengths and areas where you need to focus

Your PreACT Diagnostic Results

Once you complete your PreACT Diagnostic test, you will be taken to the results page (see figure 1.1), where you can see the number of questions you answered correctly out of the total number of questions.

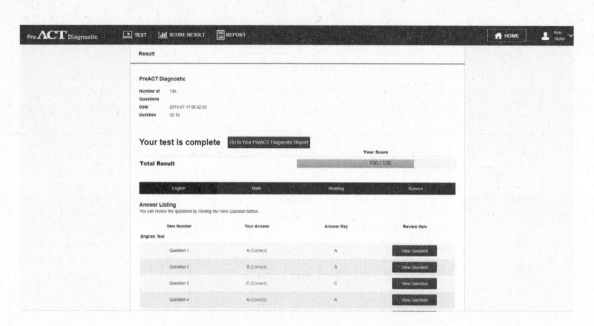

Figure 1.1: Results Page (Main)

This page allows you to go into each test section (English, math, reading, and science) and see each section question along with your answer and the correct answer (in the Answer Key column). From here, you can click on View Question to see the question and answer choices (see figure 1.2).

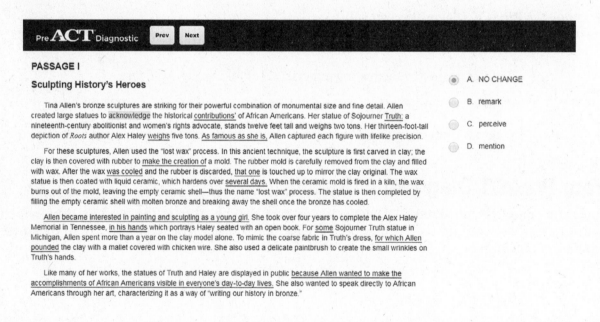

Figure 1.2: View Question Page

You can also navigate to your PreACT Diagnostic Score Report from the results page (click on Go to Your PreACT Diagnostic Report).

Your PreACT Diagnostic Score Report

Your PreACT Diagnostic Score Report (see figure 1.3) is very similar to the ACT Student Report. You can print this report and use it as you continue to prepare for the ACT.

Your PreACT Diagnostic Report

Your PreACT Diagnostic score results are ready and can be reviewed below.
You can print out the reports by clicking the 'Print' button on the left hand side.

    Print

‹ 1 2 3

Name : Ann Taylor
Test Date: July 17, 2019
SCHOOL CODE : 7
Grade: 10

Pre **ACT** Diagnostic

Student Report

Your PreACT Diagnostic® Composite Score is 23

This graph visually represents your PreACT Diagnostic scores compared to the ACT Benchmark. When looking at this you can see where your score compares to the ACT College Readiness Benchmarks.

— Your PreACT Diagnostic* Score

▢ Your PreACT Diagnostic Score Range

—●— ACT Readiness Benchmark

Your PreACT Diagnostic scores consist of different scores for each subject test (math, science, English, and reading) along with the average of all of your subject scores (the Composite score). The STEM score is the average of your math and science scores only.

Your PreACT Diagnostic Score Range

| 23 COMPOSITE | 18 MATH | 26 SCIENCE | 22 STEM | 26 ENGLISH | 23 READING |

Figure 1.3: Your PreACT Diagnostic Score Report

What Do Your Scores Mean?

The first section of the report shows your PreACT Diagnostic Composite Score, which is simply the weighted average of your English, math, reading, and science test scores. The Composite score shows how well you did on the entire test.

- STEM score: Your STEM score is the average of the math and science test scores.

- Scale score: Your scores are between 1 (the lowest you can receive) and 35 (the highest you can receive). We take the number of questions answered correctly on each section and translate it into a scale score between 1 and 35. This scale score is aligned with the 1–36 ACT score.

- Score ranges: The colored boxes on the graph below your scores are your score ranges. The heavy line within the score range is your calculated scale score, and the light gray lines with numbers are your ACT Readiness Benchmarks. You can compare your PreACT Diagnostic score ranges to the benchmarks to see if you are on track to be ready for first-year college courses.

Your Predicted ACT Score Ranges

Figure 1.4 shows your Predicted ACT Composite and subject score ranges.

Your Predicted ACT Composite Score Range is 24–27

The score below predict your future performance ranges when taking the full ACT in a year's time assuming typical achievement growth.

24–27	18–23	25–30	23–25	27–32	23–28
COMPOSITE	MATH	SCIENCE	STEM	ENGLISH	READING

Figure 1.4: Score Ranges

PreACT Diagnostic is typically taken a year or so prior to taking the ACT. Your PreACT Diagnostic scores can be used to help predict how you are likely to do if you take the ACT after an additional year of academic growth. You can use these predicted score ranges to see whether you are on track to achieve the scores you want on the ACT later in high school.

Your Detailed Results

Below your Predicted ACT Score ranges, you will find a list of the reporting categories covered in each of the four PreACT subject sections (English, math, reading, and science) (see figure 1.5). Next to each category, you will see the number of questions that you got right out of the total number of questions for the category. The bar graph enables you to easily see which categories are your strongest and weakest. This information will help you to determine areas you may need to improve in order to achieve the ACT score you want in the future.

Your Detailed PreACT Diagnostic Results

The scores below represent your performance on reporting categories measured by the test. Reporting category designations are provided to help you to start to focus on strengths and weaknesses. Categories with only a few items may be less representative of your overall achievement in that category.

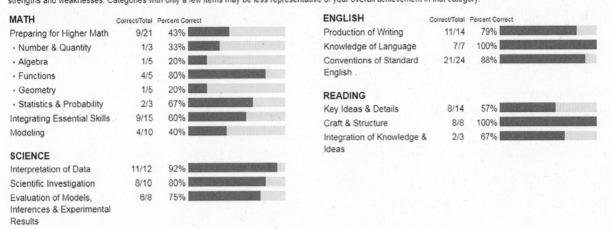

MATH	Correct/Total	Percent Correct
Preparing for Higher Math	9/21	43%
• Number & Quantity	1/3	33%
• Algebra	1/5	20%
• Functions	4/5	80%
• Geometry	1/5	20%
• Statistics & Probability	2/3	67%
Integrating Essential Skills	9/15	60%
Modeling	4/10	40%

SCIENCE	Correct/Total	Percent Correct
Interpretation of Data	11/12	92%
Scientific Investigation	8/10	80%
Evaluation of Models, Inferences & Experimental Results	6/8	75%

ENGLISH	Correct/Total	Percent Correct
Production of Writing	11/14	79%
Knowledge of Language	7/7	100%
Conventions of Standard English	21/24	88%

READING	Correct/Total	Percent Correct
Key Ideas & Details	8/14	57%
Craft & Structure	8/8	100%
Integration of Knowledge & Ideas	2/3	67%

Figure 1.5: Detailed Results

Building Your Skills

The remainder of your report, Your Item Response Analysis, is similar to the results page. Here you will see the correct response to each question in addition to any incorrect answers you may have given. You will also see some ideas for progress for each category. The descriptions and suggestions are based on your own scores and are provided to help you build on your skills in each subject area.

Name : Ann Taylor
Test Date: July 17, 2019
SCHOOL CODE : 7

Pre**ACT** Diagnostic

Student Report

Your Item Response Analysis

Ask for your test booklet so you can review the questions and your answers. Ideas for Progress are based on your scores. The improvement suggestions provided are a sample of the Ideas for Progress for your subject scale score. Your particular profile of strengths and weaknesses will influence which suggestions are most relevant for you. More information can be found at www.act.org/standards/ideasforprogress

MATH

Correctly Answered: 18 of 36
Omitted: 0 of 36
Incorrectly Answered: 18 of 36

Question	Correct Answer	Incorrect Response	Question	Correct Answer	Incorrect Response
1	C		21	A	•
2	E		22	E	•
3	E		23	D	
4	C		24	E	
5	A	•	25	B	•
6	C		26	C	•
7	C		27	E	
8	B	•	28	C	
9	A		29	C	•
10	D		30	D	•
11	D		31	D	•
12	C	•	32	E	•
13	B	•	33	D	•
14	C		34	A	
15	B	•	35	A	•
16	E	•	36	C	
17	A	•			
18	B	•			
19	A				
20	E				

Ideas for Progress

Number & Quantity

• recognize, identify, and apply basic properties of real numbers. (e.g. commutative, associative, identities)

Algebra

• evaluate algebraic expressions and solve simple equations, using integers for Algebra

Functions

• use function notation to create equations that model real-world and mathematical problems

Geometry

• find area and perimeter of triangles and rectangles by substituting given values into standard geometric formulas

Statistics & Probability

• gather, organize, display, and analyze data in a variety of ways for use in problem solving

SCIENCE

Figure 1.6: Item Response Analysis

After taking PreACT Diagnostic, you now

• Have been exposed to the types of questions and content featured on the ACT test

• Have been exposed to the experience of taking the ACT test

• Have a prediction of how you are likely to perform on the ACT test

• Have an understanding of your strengths and areas where you need to focus

• Are ready to continue your preparation for the ACT with helpful information regarding what you know and what you need to learn

Chapter 2:
About the ACT

The ACT measures your achievement in core academic areas important for your college and career success: English, math, reading, science, and (optionally) writing. It isn't an IQ test—it doesn't measure your basic intelligence. It's an achievement test that's been carefully designed—using surveys of classroom teachers, reviews of curriculum guides for schools all over the country, and advice from curriculum specialists and college faculty members—to be one of several effective tools for evaluating your college and career readiness.

The individual tests that make up the ACT consist of questions that measure your knowledge and skills. You're not required to memorize facts or vocabulary to do well on the ACT. Of course, all the terms, formulas, and other information you learned in your classes will be useful to you when you take the ACT. However, last-minute cramming (such as memorizing 5,000 vocabulary words or the entire periodic table of elements) won't directly improve your performance on the ACT.

Description of the Full ACT Test

The full ACT consists of four multiple-choice tests—English, mathematics, reading, and science—and an optional writing test. Topics covered on these five tests correspond very closely to topics covered in typical high school classes. Table 1.1 gives you a snapshot of all five tests.

Test	Questions	Time	Content Covered
Table 1.1: ACT Tests			
English	75 questions	45 minutes	Measures standard written English knowledge and skills along with English language conventions
Mathematics	60 questions	60 minutes	Measures mathematical skills students have typically acquired in courses taken up to the beginning of grade 12
Reading	40 questions	35 minutes	Measures reading comprehension
Science	40 questions	35 minutes	Measures the interpretation, analysis, evaluation, reasoning, and problem-solving skills required in the natural sciences
Writing (optional)	1 prompt	40 minutes	Measures writing skills emphasized in high school English classes and in entry-level college composition courses

Questions on the tests are intended to help assess college and career readiness. The following sections provide an overview of what you should know to perform well on each test. For additional details, check out the ACT College and Career Readiness Standards presented in chapter 5.

English Test

75 questions, 45 minutes

The English test consists of five essays or passages, each of which is accompanied by a sequence of multiple-choice test questions. Different passage types are employed to provide a variety of rhetorical situations. Passages are chosen not only for their appropriateness in assessing writing skills but also to reflect students' interests and experiences.

You will receive four scores for the ACT English test: a total test score based on all 75 questions and three reporting category scores based on the following:

- Production of Writing

- Knowledge of Language

- Conventions of Standard English

Production of Writing

Production of Writing tests knowledge and skills in two areas of English composition:

- Topic development in terms of purpose and focus

- Organization, unity, and cohesion

Topic Development in Terms of Purpose and Focus

Examples of knowledge and skills tested include the following:

- Determine the relevance of material to the topic or the focus of the passage or paragraph.

- Identify the purpose of a word or phrase (for example, identify a person, define a term, or describe an object).

- Determine whether a passage has met a specific goal.

- Use a word, phrase, or sentence to accomplish a specific purpose, such as convey a feeling or attitude or illustrate a given statement.

Organization, Unity, and Cohesion

Examples of knowledge and skills tested include the following:

- Determine the need for transition words or phrases to define relationships in terms of time or logic.

- Determine the most logical place for a sentence in a paragraph.

- Provide a suitable conclusion for a paragraph or passage (for example, summarizing the main idea).

- Provide a suitable introduction for a paragraph or passage.

- Rearrange sentences in a paragraph or paragraphs in a passage to establish a logical flow.

- Determine the most logical place to divide a paragraph to achieve the stated goal.

Knowledge of Language

Knowledge of Language questions test your ability to clearly and succinctly express yourself in written English. Knowledge and skills tested include the following:

- Revise unclear, clumsy, and confusing writing.

- Delete redundant and wordy material.

- Revise an expression to make it conform to the style and tone used throughout the passage.

- Determine the need for conjunctions to create logical connections between clauses.

- Choose the most appropriate word or phrase in terms of the sentence content.

Conventions of Standard English

Conventions of Standard English questions test knowledge and skills such as the following:

- Determine the need for punctuation or conjunctions to join clauses or to correct awkward-sounding fragments, fused sentences, and faulty subordination and coordination of clauses.

- Recognize and correct inappropriate shifts in verb tense.

- Recognize and correct disturbances in sentence structure, such as faulty placement of adjectives, participial phrase fragments, missing or incorrect relative pronouns, dangling or misplaced modifiers, faulty parallelism, run-on sentences, and weak conjunctions between independent clauses.

- Maintain consistent and logical verb tense and voice and pronoun person within a paragraph or passage.

Note: Spelling, vocabulary, and rote recall of grammar rules are not tested.

Mathematics Test

60 questions, 60 minutes

The mathematics test presents multiple-choice questions that require you to use reasoning skills to solve practical math problems. The material covered on the test emphasizes the major content areas that are prerequisites to successful performance in entry-level courses in college mathematics. Some questions may belong to a set of several questions (for example, several questions about the same graph or chart).

Conceptual knowledge and computational skills are assumed as background for the problems, but recall of complex formulas and extensive computation is not required.

Nine scores are reported for the ACT mathematics test: a total test score based on all 60 questions and eight reporting category scores based on specific mathematical knowledge and skills. The reporting categories are:

- Preparing for Higher Mathematics, which includes separate scores for Number and Quantity, Algebra, Functions, Geometry, and Statistics and Probability

- Integrating Essential Skills

- Modeling

Preparing for Higher Mathematics

This category captures the more recent mathematics that students are learning, starting when they begin using algebra as a general way of expressing and solving equations. This category is divided into the following five subcategories:

- Number and Quantity

- Algebra

- Functions

- Geometry

- Statistics and Probability

Number and Quantity

Math questions in this category test your knowledge of numbers and fundamental math concepts and operations, including the following:

- Perform calculations on whole numbers and decimals.

- Recognize equivalent fractions and fractions in lowest terms.

- Locate rational numbers (whole numbers, fractions, decimals, and mixed numbers) on the number line.

- Recognize single-digit factors of a number.

- Identify a digit's place value.

- Demonstrate knowledge of elementary number concepts, including rounding, ordering of decimals, pattern identification, primes, and greatest common factor.

- Write powers of 10 using exponents.

- Comprehend the concept of length on the number line, and find the distance between two points.

- Understand absolute value in terms of distance.

- Find the distance between two points with the same x-coordinate or y-coordinate in the coordinate plane.

- Add, subtract, and multiply matrices (tables of numbers).

- Order fractions.

- Find and use the least common multiple.

- Demonstrate knowledge of complex numbers and multiply two complex numbers.

- Comprehend the concept of irrational numbers, such as π.

- Apply properties of rational exponents.

- Use relations involving addition, subtraction, and scalar multiplication of vectors and matrices.

- Analyze and draw conclusions based on number concepts.

Algebra and Functions

The mathematics test contains questions that require knowledge of and skills in algebra, functions, or both. *Algebra* involves formulas and equations in which letters and other symbols are used to represent unknown or unspecified values. A *function* is a rule, equation, or expression that produces exactly one output for any given input; for example, $2x$ is a function in that any input used for x results in an output that is twice the input's value.

Algebra

Algebra knowledge and skills tested include the following:

- Demonstrate knowledge of basic expressions, such as $b + g$ to identify a total.

- Solve equations in the form $x + a = b$, where a and b are whole numbers or decimals.

- Use substitution to evaluate mathematical expressions.

- Combine like terms, such as $2x + 5x$.

- Add and subtract algebraic expressions.

- Multiply two binomials.

- Match inequalities with their graphs on the number line.

- Demonstrate knowledge of slope.

- Solve real-world problems by using first-degree equations.

- Solve inequalities.

- Match linear or compound inequalities with their graphs on the number line.

- Add, subtract, and multiply polynomials.

- Solve quadratic equations.

- Factor quadratics.

- Work with squares/square roots and cubes/cube roots of numbers.

- Work with scientific notation.

- Solve problems involving positive integer exponents.

- Determine the slope of a line from an equation.

- Solve linear inequalities when the method involves reversing the inequality sign.

- Solve systems of two linear equations.

- Solve absolute value equations and inequalities.

- Match quadratic inequalities with their graphs on the number line.

Functions

Questions that involve functions test your ability to do the following:

- Understand the concept of a function having a well-defined output value at each valid input value.

- Extend a given pattern by a few terms for patterns that have a constant increase or decrease between terms or that have a constant factor between terms.

- Evaluate linear, quadratic, and polynomial functions expressed in function notation at the integer level.

- Interpret statements that use function notation in terms of their context.

- Find the domain of polynomial functions and rational functions.

- Find the range of polynomial functions.

- Find where a rational function's graph has a vertical asymptote.

- Use function notation for simple functions of two variables.

- Relate a graph to a situation described qualitatively in terms of faster change or slower change.

- Build functions for relations that are inversely proportional or exponential.

- Find a recursive expression for the general term in a sequence described recursively.

- Evaluate composite functions of integer values.

- Compare actual values and the values of a modeling function to judge model fit and compare models.

- Demonstrate knowledge of geometric sequences.

- Demonstrate knowledge of unit circle trigonometry.

- Match graphs of basic trigonometric functions with their equations.

- Use trigonometric concepts and basic identities to solve problems.

- Demonstrate knowledge of logarithms.

- Write an expression for the composite of two simple functions.

Algebra and Functions

Questions that involve both algebra and functions test your ability to do the following:

- Solve problems using whole numbers and decimals in the context of money.

- Solve one- or two-step arithmetic problems using positive rational numbers, such as percent.

- Relate a graph to a situation described quantitatively.

- Solve two- or three-step arithmetic problems involving concepts such as rate and proportion, sales tax, percentage off, and estimation.

- Perform word-to-symbol translations.

- Solve multistep arithmetic problems that involve planning or converting units of measure (for example, feet per second to miles per hour).

- Build functions and write expressions, equations, or inequalities with a single variable for common pre-algebra settings, such as rate and distance problems and problems that involve proportions.

- Match linear equations with their graphs in the coordinate plane.

- Solve word problems containing several rates, proportions, or percentages.

- Build functions and write expressions, equations, and inequalities for common algebra settings.

- Interpret and use information from graphs in the coordinate plane.

- Solve complex math problems involving percent of increase or decrease or requiring integration of several concepts.

- Build functions and write expressions, equations, and inequalities when the process requires planning and/or strategic manipulation.

- Analyze and draw conclusions based on properties of algebra and/or functions.

- Analyze and draw conclusions based on information from graphs in the coordinate plane.

- Identify characteristics of graphs based on a set of conditions or on a general equation such as $y = ax^2 + c$.

- Given an equation or function, find an equation or function whose graph is a translation by specified amounts up or down.

Geometry

Geometry questions are based primarily on the mathematical properties and relationships of points, lines, angles, two-dimensional shapes, and three-dimensional objects. Knowledge and skills tested include the following:

- Estimate the length of a line segment based on other lengths in a geometric figure.

- Calculate the length of a line segment based on the lengths of other line segments that go in the same direction (for example, overlapping line segments and parallel sides of polygons with only right angles).

- Perform common conversions of money and of length, weight, mass, and time within a measurement system (for example, inches to feet and hours to minutes).

- Compute the area and perimeter of triangles, rectangles, and other polygons.

- Use properties of parallel lines to find the measure of an angle.

- Exhibit knowledge of basic angle properties and special sums of angle measures (for example, 90°, 180°, and 360°).

- Use geometric formulas when all necessary information is given.

- Locate points in the coordinate plane.

- Translate points up, down, left, and right in the coordinate plane.

- Use several angle properties to find an unknown angle measure.

- Count the number of lines of symmetry of a geometric figure.

- Use symmetry of isosceles triangles to find unknown side lengths or angle measures.

- Recognize that real-world measurements are typically imprecise and that an appropriate level of precision is related to the measuring device and procedure.

- Compute the perimeter of composite geometric figures with unknown side lengths.

- Compute the area and circumference of circles.

- Given the length of two sides of a right triangle, find the length of the third side.

- Express the sine, cosine, and tangent of an angle in a right triangle as a ratio of given side lengths.

- Determine the slope of a line from points or a graph.

- Find the midpoint of a line segment.

- Find the coordinates of a point rotated 180° around a given center point.

- Use relationships involving area, perimeter, and volume of geometric figures to compute another measure (for example, surface area for a cube of a given volume and simple geometric probability).

- Use the Pythagorean theorem.

- Apply properties of 30°–60°–90°, 45°–45°–90°, similar, and congruent triangles.

- Apply basic trigonometric ratios to solve right-triangle problems.

- Use the distance formula.

- Use properties of parallel and perpendicular lines to determine an equation of a line or coordinates of a point.

- Find the coordinates of a point reflected across a vertical or horizontal line or across $y = x$.

- Find the coordinates of a point rotated 90° across a vertical.

- Recognize special characteristics of parabolas and circles (for example, the vertex of a parabola and the center or radius of a circle).

- Use relationships among angles, arcs, and distances in a circle.

- Compute the area of composite geometric figures when planning and/or visualization is required.

- Use scale factors to determine the magnitude of a size change.

- Analyze and draw conclusions based on a set of conditions.

- Solve multistep geometry problems that involve integrating concepts, planning, and/or visualization.

Statistics and Probability

Statistics is a branch of mathematics that involves the collection and analysis of large quantities of numerical data. *Probability* is a branch of mathematics that involves calculating the likelihood of an event occurring or a condition existing. Statistics and Probability questions test your ability to do the following:

- Calculate averages.

- Read and extract relevant data from a basic table or chart and use the data in a computation.

- Use the relationship between the probability of an event and the probability of its complement.

- Calculate the missing data value given the average and all other data values.

- Translate from one representation of data to another (for example, from a bar graph to a circle graph).

- Compute probabilities.

- Describe events as combinations of other events (for example, using *and*, *or*, and *not*).

- Demonstrate knowledge of and apply counting techniques.

- Calculate the average given the frequency counts of all the data values.

- Manipulate data from tables and charts.

- Use Venn diagrams in counting.

- Recognize that when data summaries are reported in the real world, results are often rounded and must be interpreted as having appropriate precision.

- Recognize that when a statistical model is used, model values typically differ from actual values.

- Calculate or use a weighted average.

- Interpret and use information from tables and charts, including two-way frequency tables.

- Recognize the concepts of conditional and joint probability and of independence expressed in real-world contexts.

- Distinguish among mean, median, and mode for a list of numbers.

- Analyze and draw conclusions based on information from tables and charts, including two-way frequency tables.

- Understand the role of randomization in surveys, experiments, and observational studies.

- Demonstrate knowledge of conditional and joint probability.

- Recognize that part of the power of statistical modeling comes from looking at regularity in the differences between actual values and model values.

Integrating Essential Skills

Students learn some of the most useful mathematics before grade 8: rates and percentages; proportional relationships; area, surface area, and volume; average and median; expressing numbers in different ways; using expressions to represent quantities and equations to capture relationships; and other topics. Each year, students should grow in what they can accomplish using learning from prior years. Students should be able to solve problems of increasing complexity, combine skills in longer chains of steps, apply skills in more varied contexts, understand more connections, and increase fluency. In order to assess whether students have had appropriate growth, all questions in this reporting category focus on the higher-level cognitive skills, such as making decisions on how to approach a problem, comparing, reasoning, planning, applying algebra strategically, drawing conclusions, solving novel problems, and the like.

Modeling

Modeling uses mathematics to represent with a model an analysis of an actual, empirical situation. Models often help us predict or understand the actual. However, sometimes knowledge of the actual helps us understand the model, such as when addition is introduced to students as a model of combining two groups. The Modeling reporting category represents all questions that involve producing, interpreting, understanding, evaluating, and improving models. Each modeling question is also counted in the other appropriate reporting categories previously identified. Thus, the Modeling reporting category is an overall measure of how well a student uses modeling skills across mathematical topics.

Reading Test

40 questions, 35 minutes

The reading test comprises four sections, each containing one long or two shorter prose passages that are representative of the level and kinds of text commonly encountered in first-year college curricula. Passages on topics in social studies, natural science, literary narrative (including prose fiction), and the humanities are included, and the passages vary in terms of how challenging and complex they are.

Four scores are reported for the ACT reading test: a total test score based on all 40 questions and three reporting category scores based on specific knowledge and skills.

The reading test measures your reading comprehension in three general areas:

- Key Ideas and Details
- Craft and Structure
- Integration of Knowledge and Ideas

Key Ideas and Details

Questions that test reading comprehension focus primarily on identifying key details in the passage and grasping the overall meaning of the passage. Reading skills tested are divided into three categories:

- Close reading
- Central ideas, themes, and summaries
- Relationships

Close Reading

Close-reading skills involve your ability to do the following:

- Locate and interpret facts or details in a passage.

- Draw logical conclusions.

- Paraphrase statements.

Central Ideas, Themes, and Summaries

Questions that focus on central ideas, themes, and summaries challenge your ability to do the following:

- Identify the topic and distinguish it from the central idea or theme.

- Identify or infer the central idea or theme of a passage.

- Summarize key supporting ideas or details.

Relationships

Relationship questions involve the ability to do the following:

- Identify the sequence of events or place events in their correct sequence.

- Identify stated or implied cause-effect relationships.

- Identify stated or implied comparative relationships.

Craft and Structure

Some reading questions go beyond the meaning of the passage to challenge your understanding of how the author crafted and structured the passage. Reading skills tested in this area are divided into three categories:

- Word meanings and word choice

- Text structure

- Purpose and point of view

Word Meanings and Word Choice

Reading questions may focus on the meaning or impact of a word or phrase, challenging your ability to do the following:

- Interpret the meaning of a word or phrase, including determining technical, academic, connotative, and figurative meanings.

- Understand the implication of a word or phrase and of descriptive language.

- Analyze how the choice of a specific word or phrase shapes the meaning or tone of a passage.

Text Structure

Text-structure questions ask you to analyze how various structural elements function to serve a specific purpose in the passage. To answer such questions, you may need to do one of the following:

- Analyze how one or more sentences in passages relate to the whole passage.

- Identify or infer the function of one or more paragraphs.

- Analyze the overall structure of a passage.

Purpose and Point of View

The reading test may include questions that challenge your ability to do the following:

- Identify or infer the author's or narrator's purpose or intent.

- Determine how an author's or narrator's purpose or intent shapes the content and style of the passage.

- Recognize an author's or narrator's point of view.

Integration of Knowledge and Ideas

Reading questions may require that you go beyond simply reading and understanding a passage to analyzing one or more passages. Reading skills tested in the area of Integration of Knowledge and Ideas are divided into two categories:

- Arguments

- Multiple texts

Arguments

Questions related to argumentative essays may test your ability to do the following:

- Identify or infer the central claim being presented in the passage.

- Analyze how one or more sentences offer reasons for or support the claim.

Multiple Texts

Multiple-text questions involve reading two passages and doing the following:

- Compare the two passages.

- Draw logical conclusions using information from the two passages.

Science Test

40 questions, 35 minutes

The science test measures the interpretation, analysis, evaluation, reasoning, and problem-solving skills required in the natural sciences: life science/biology; physical science/chemistry, physics; and earth and space science. (See chapter 5 for a more detailed breakdown of science content covered on the test.)

The test assumes that students are in the process of taking the core science course of study (three years or more) that will prepare them for college-level work and have completed a course in earth science and/or physical science and a course in biology. The test presents several sets of scientific information, each followed by a number of multiple-choice test questions. The scientific information is conveyed in the form of reading passages and graphic representations—graphs (charts), tables, and illustrations.

Four scores are reported for the ACT science test: a total test score based on all 40 questions and three reporting category scores based on scientific knowledge, skills, and practices. The reporting categories are:

- Interpretation of Data
- Scientific Investigation
- Evaluation of Models, Inferences, and Experimental Results

Interpretation of Data

Interpretation of Data involves the following skills:

- Select data from a data presentation (for example, a food web diagram, a graph, a table, or a phase diagram).
- Identify features of a table, graph, or diagram (for example, units of measurement).
- Find information in text that describes a data presentation.
- Understand scientific terminology.
- Determine how the values of variables change as the value of another variable changes in a data presentation.
- Compare or combine data from one or more data presentations (for example, order or sum data from a table).
- Translate information into a table, graph, or diagram.
- Perform a interpolation or extrapolation using data in a table or graph (for example, categorize data from a table using a scale from another table).
- Determine and/or use a mathematical relationship that exists between data.
- Analyze presented information when given new information.

Scientific Investigation

Questions that apply to scientific investigation are typically related to experiments and other research. Such questions challenge your ability to do the following:

- Find information in text that describes an experiment.

- Understand the tools and functions of tools used in an experiment.

- Understand the methods used in an experiment.

- Understand experimental design.

- Identify a control in an experiment.

- Identify similarities and differences between experiments.

- Determine which experiments use a given tool, method, or aspect of design.

- Predict the results of an additional trial or measurement in an experiment.

- Determine the experimental conditions that would produce specified results.

- Determine the hypothesis for an experiment.

- Determine an alternate method for testing a hypothesis.

- Understand precision and accuracy issues.

- Predict the effects of modifying the design or methods of an experiment.

- Determine which additional trial or experiment could be performed to enhance or evaluate experimental results.

Evaluation of Models, Inferences, and Experimental Results

Some questions on the science test challenge your ability to evaluate models, inferences, and experimental results. (A *model* is a description of an object or phenomenon intended to explain and predict its behavior.) To answer such questions, you must be able to do the following:

- Find basic information in a model.

- Identify implications in a model.

- Determine which models present certain information.

- Determine which hypothesis, prediction, or conclusion is, or is not, consistent with one or more data presentations, models, or pieces of information in text.

- Identify key assumptions in a model.

- Identify similarities and differences between models.

- Determine whether presented information or new information supports or contradicts (or weakens) a hypothesis or conclusion and why.

- Identify the strengths and weaknesses of models.

- Determine which models are supported or weakened by new information.

- Determine which experimental results or models support or contradict a hypothesis, prediction, or conclusion.

- Use new information to make a prediction based on a model.

Writing Test (Optional)

1 prompt, 40 minutes

The writing test is a 40-minute essay test that measures your writing skills—specifically those writing skills emphasized in high school English classes and in entry-level college composition courses.

The test asks you to produce an essay in response to a contemporary issue. You will be given a prompt that presents the issue and provides three different perspectives on it. Your task is to write an essay in which you develop a perspective on the issue and explore how it relates to at least one other perspective.

Trained readers will evaluate your essay for the evidence it provides of a number of core writing skills. You will receive a total of five scores for this test: a single subject-level writing score reported on a scale of 2–12 and four domain scores based on an analytic scoring rubric. The four domain scores are

- Ideas and Analysis

- Development and Support

- Organization

- Language Use and Conventions

Ideas and Analysis

Effective writing depends on effective ideas. It is important to think carefully about the issue in the prompt and compose an argument that addresses the issue meaningfully. In evaluating the ideas and analysis in your essay, readers will look for your ability to do the following:

- Generate a clear main idea that establishes your perspective on the issue.

- Engage with multiple perspectives on the issue by analyzing the relationship between your perspective and at least one other perspective.

- Clarify your understanding of the issue and differing perspectives on it by providing a relevant context for discussion.

- Analyze critical elements (e.g., implications and complexities) of the issue and perspectives under consideration.

Development and Support

Even the best ideas must be developed and supported to be effective in a written argument. By explaining and illustrating your points, you help the reader understand your thinking. In evaluating this dimension of your essay, readers will look for your ability to do the following:

- Clarify your ideas by explaining your reasoning.

- Bolster your claims with persuasive examples.

- Convey the significance of your perspective by exploring reasons why your ideas are worth considering.

- Extend your argument by considering qualifications, exceptions, counterarguments, and complicating factors.

Organization

Organizational choices are essential to effective writing. Guide the reader through your discussion by arranging your ideas according to the logic of your argument. As readers evaluate the organization of your essay, they will look for your ability to do the following:

- Unify your essay by making strategic use of a controlling idea and other organizational techniques (e.g., theme or motif).

- Group ideas clearly, with each paragraph limited to the discussion of related ideas.

- Produce a sequence of ideas that follows a clear logic, both in terms of the argument's overall structure (e.g., introduction, body, conclusion) and within the argument itself, with each point following from the last.

- Use transitions to connect ideas, both within paragraphs (e.g., relating claims to support) and across paragraphs (e.g., moving from one discussion into another).

Language Use and Conventions

Skillful language use enhances argumentative writing. Strategic choices in the vocabulary you use and the style you employ can make your essay more effective. To evaluate your use of language, readers will look for your ability to do the following:

- Make precise word choices that communicate your ideas with clarity.

- Demonstrate control over a variety of sentence structures.

- Match the style of your writing to the audience and purpose (e.g., more evocative language to convey emotional appeals versus a more neutral voice to convey an argument based on reason).

- Accurately apply the conventions of grammar, word usage, syntax, and mechanics.

The Fifth Test and Section Retesting

ACT is dedicated to meeting professional testing standards. To accomplish this, ACT includes additional questions on the test that do not count toward your score. This practice ensures that ACT develops questions that are fair and of the highest possible quality.

If you are taking the full ACT test, your room supervisor will ask you to take a 20-minute fifth test that includes these additional questions.

If you are taking a section retest, the additional questions are blended in with the questions that count toward your score. The timing for the section retest accommodates these additional questions.

ACT Test Formats: Paper and Online

The ACT is available as a paper test and as an online test in certain states and educational districts. Beginning in September 2020, students taking the ACT test on a national test date will have the option to take the test online or to take a paper test. Regardless of format, what is most important is the knowledge and skills you have developed over your course of study. If you know the material, whether you choose answers by marking them on paper or clicking an option on a computer screen will likely make little difference. Beginning in September 2020, students who take the national test, and have a Composite score on file with ACT, will be presented with the option to take an ACT section retest. After taking a full exam at least one time, students will have the option to narrow their focus and prepare for individual section tests rather than studying for all test subjects.

ACT section tests will give students a chance to retest and make an effort to master content they have not yet shown mastery in, thereby increasing the likelihood of improving their superscore that will be shared with colleges and universities.

Students will be able to take up to three individual section tests on national test days if they chose to take a section retest. The writing test can be one of the sections, even if the student has never taken writing before.

Using a Calculator

You may use a permitted calculator only on the mathematics test, but you are not required to do so. All math problems on the test can be solved without a calculator, and you may be able to perform some of the math more quickly in your head or on scratch paper.

Note: You may use any four-function, scientific, or graphing calculator as long as it is a permitted calculator modified, if necessary, as described in the following. For additional details and ACT's most current calculator policy, visit www.act.org.

Certain types of calculators, including the following, are prohibited:

- Calculators with built-in or downloaded computer algebra system (CAS) functionality, including the TI-89, TI-92, TI-Nspire CAS, HP Prime, HP 48GII, HP 40G, HP 49G, HP 50G, fx-ClassPad 400, ClassPad 300, ClassPad 330, and all

Casio models that start with CFX-9970G. (Using the TI-89 is the most common reason students are dismissed from the ACT for prohibited calculator use.)

- Handheld, tablet, or laptop computers, including PDAs.

- Electronic writing pads or pen-input devices (the Sharp EL 9600 is permitted).

- Calculators built into cell phones or any other electronic communication devices.

- Calculators with a typewriter keypad (letter keys in QWERTY format, but letter keys not in QWERTY format are permitted).

The following types of calculators are permitted but only after they are modified as noted:

- Calculators that can hold programs or documents (remove all documents and all programs that have CAS functionality).

- Calculators with paper tape (remove the tape).

- Calculators that make noise (mute the device).

- Calculators with an infrared data port (completely cover the infrared data port with heavy opaque material such as duct tape or electrician's tape). These calculators include the Hewlett-Packard HP 38G series, HP 39G series, and HP 48G.

- Calculators that have power cords (remove all power and electrical cords).

- Accessible calculators (such as audio-talking or braille calculators) may be allowed under the accessibility policies for the ACT test. (Visit www.act.org for details.)

If you choose to use a calculator during the mathematics test, follow these guidelines:

- Use a calculator you are accustomed to using. A more powerful, but unfamiliar, calculator may be a disadvantage. If you are unaccustomed to using a calculator, practice using it when you take the practice test in this book, so you are comfortable with using it in a test situation.

- Sharing calculators during the test is not permitted.

- Make sure your calculator works properly. If your calculator uses batteries, the batteries should be strong enough to last throughout the testing session.

- Bring a spare calculator and/or extra batteries.

Taking the Test

Knowing what to expect on test day can alleviate any anxiety you may feel. The following list describes the steps you will take through the testing day:

1. You must report to the test center by the reporting time.

   - If you are testing on a *national test* date and are taking the full ACT test, the reporting time is 8:00 AM. If you are taking a section test on a *national test* date, please check your admission ticket for your reporting time.

     ○ You will need to bring the following:

       – A printed copy of your ACT admission ticket, which contains important match information that cannot be found anywhere else. Failure to bring your admission ticket will prevent you from being able to test.

       – Acceptable photo ID; if you do not bring acceptable photo ID, you will not be allowed to take the test.

       – Sharpened no. 2 soft-lead pencils with good erasers (no mechanical pencils or ink pens).

       – If you are taking the ACT test online, scratch paper will be provided for you.

       – A calculator, if you would like to use one.

   - If you are testing during the week day at your school through *state and district* testing the reporting time will be at the same time you usually report for school.

     ○ You will need to bring the following:

       – Acceptable photo ID

       – Sharpened no. 2 soft-lead pencils with good erasers (no mechanical pencils or ink pens)

       – A calculator, if you would like to use one

   (**Note:** You will *not* be admitted to test if you are late or if your ID does not meet ACT's requirements.)

2. When all examinees present at the reporting time are checked in and seated, wait until you are notified to start the test.

3. A short break is scheduled after the first two tests. You are prohibited from using a cell phone or any electronic device during the break, and you may not eat or drink anything in the test room. (If you take the ACT with writing, you will have time before the writing test to relax and sharpen your pencils.)

4. When time has expired, paper tests are collected. Online tests must be submitted prior to your dismissal.

Note: If you do not complete all your tests for any reason, tell a member of the testing staff whether or not you want your answer document or online test to be scored before you leave the test center. If you do not, all tests attempted will be scored.

NOTES

3

Chapter 3:
Taking a Practice Test

In this chapter, you'll find a practice ACT test, copies of real answer documents for recording your answers, and explanatory answers for the questions on all of the multiple-choice tests.

The practice test features the contents of the tests in the same order as they will be on the ACT: the English test, the mathematics test, the reading test, the science test, and the optional writing test. Following the complete practice test, you will find the explanatory answers for the multiple-choice questions in the same pattern as the individual tests (English, mathematics, reading, and science).

Two copies of the answer documents that you can tear out and use to record your answers for the multiple-choice tests precede each practice test. (Two copies of these answer documents have been provided in case you make errors or if you would like to retake the practice test. When you take the actual ACT test, however, only one answer document will be provided.) One copy of the writing test answer document, which you can tear out (or photocopy) and use to write your essay, is provided for the practice writing test.

Simulating Testing Conditions

We recommend that you take the practice test under conditions similar to those you will experience on test day.

The ACT® Sample Answer Document

EXAMINEE STATEMENTS, CERTIFICATION, AND SIGNATURE

1. **Statements**: I understand that by registering for, launching, starting, or submitting answer documents for an ACT® test, I am agreeing to comply with and be bound by the *Terms and Conditions: Testing Rules and Policies for the ACT® Test* ("Terms").

   I UNDERSTAND AND AGREE THAT THE TERMS PERMIT ACT TO CANCEL MY SCORES IF THERE IS REASON TO BELIEVE THEY ARE INVALID. THE TERMS ALSO LIMIT DAMAGES AVAILABLE TO ME AND REQUIRE ARBITRATION. BY AGREEING TO ARBITRATION, I WAIVE MY RIGHT TO HAVE DISPUTES HEARD BY A JUDGE OR JURY.

   I understand that ACT owns the test questions and responses, and I will not share them with anyone by any form of communication before, during, or after the test administration. I understand that taking the test for someone else may violate the law and subject me to legal penalties. I consent to the collection and processing of personally identifying information I provide, and its subsequent use and disclosure, as described in the ACT Privacy Policy (www.act.org/privacy.html). I also permit ACT to transfer my personally identifying information to the United States, to ACT, or to a third-party service provider, where it will be subject to use and disclosure under the laws of the United States, including being accessible to law enforcement or national security authorities.

2. **Certification**: Copy the italicized certification below, then sign and date in the spaces provided.

   *I agree to the **Statements** above and certify that I am the person whose information appears on this form.*

   _____

   _____

   _____   _____

   Your Signature   Today's Date

Do NOT mark in this shaded area.

USE A SOFT LEAD NO. 2 PENCIL ONLY.
(Do NOT use a mechanical pencil, ink, ballpoint, correction fluid, or felt-tip pen.)

A
NAME, MAILING ADDRESS, AND TELEPHONE
(Please print.)

Last Name   First Name   MI (Middle Initial)

House Number & Street (Apt. No.); or PO Box & No.; or RR & No.

City   State/Province   ZIP/Postal Code

Area Code   Number   Country

ACT, Inc.—Confidential Restricted when data present

ALL examinees must complete block A – please print.

Blocks B, C, and D are required for all examinees. Find the MATCHING INFORMATION on your ticket. Enter it EXACTLY the same way, even if any of the information is missing or incorrect. Fill in the corresponding ovals. If you do not complete these blocks to match your previous information EXACTLY, your scores will be **delayed up to 8 weeks**.

ACT®
PO BOX 168, IOWA CITY, IA 52243-0168

B MATCH NAME
(First 5 letters of last name)

A B C D E F G H I J K L M N O P Q R S T U V W X Y Z

C MATCH NUMBER

1 2 3 4 5 6 7 8 9 0

D DATE OF BIRTH

Month	Day	Year
January		
February		
March	1	1 1
April	2	2 2
May	3	3 3
June	4	4 4
July	5	5 5
August	6	6 6
September	7	7 7
October	8	8 8
November	9	9 9
December	0	0 0

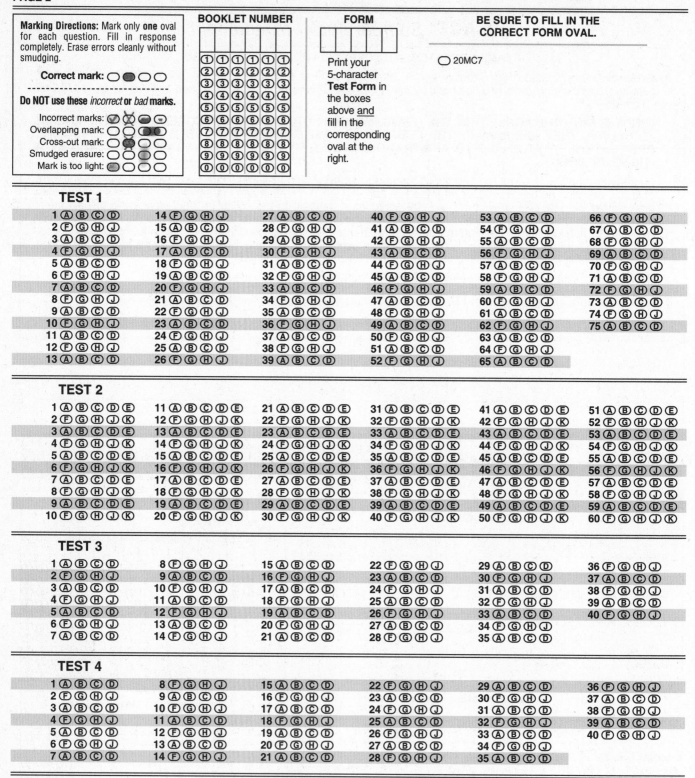

The ACT® *Sample Answer Document*

EXAMINEE STATEMENTS, CERTIFICATION, AND SIGNATURE

1. **Statements**: I understand that by registering for, launching, starting, or submitting answer documents for an ACT® test, I am agreeing to comply with and be bound by the *Terms and Conditions: Testing Rules and Policies for the ACT® Test* ("Terms").

   I UNDERSTAND AND AGREE THAT THE TERMS PERMIT ACT TO CANCEL MY SCORES IF THERE IS REASON TO BELIEVE THEY ARE INVALID. THE TERMS ALSO LIMIT DAMAGES AVAILABLE TO ME AND REQUIRE ARBITRATION. BY AGREEING TO ARBITRATION, I WAIVE MY RIGHT TO HAVE DISPUTES HEARD BY A JUDGE OR JURY.

   I understand that ACT owns the test questions and responses, and I will not share them with anyone by any form of communication before, during, or after the test administration. I understand that taking the test for someone else may violate the law and subject me to legal penalties. I consent to the collection and processing of personally identifying information I provide, and its subsequent use and disclosure, as described in the ACT Privacy Policy (www.act.org/privacy.html). I also permit ACT to transfer my personally identifying information to the United States, to ACT, or to a third-party service provider, where it will be subject to use and disclosure under the laws of the United States, including being accessible to law enforcement or national security authorities.

2. **Certification**: Copy the italicized certification below, then sign and date in the spaces provided.

   *I agree to the **Statements** above and certify that I am the person whose information appears on this form.*

   _____

   _____

   _____   _____
   Your Signature   Today's Date

Do NOT mark in this shaded area.

USE A SOFT LEAD NO. 2 PENCIL ONLY.
(Do NOT use a mechanical pencil, ink, ballpoint, correction fluid, or felt-tip pen.)

A NAME, MAILING ADDRESS, AND TELEPHONE
(Please print.)

Last Name   First Name   MI (Middle Initial)

House Number & Street (Apt. No.); or PO Box & No.; or RR & No.

City   State/Province   ZIP/Postal Code

Area Code   Number   Country

ACT, Inc.—Confidential Restricted when data present

ALL examinees must complete block A – please print.

Blocks B, C, and D are required for all examinees. Find the MATCHING INFORMATION on your ticket. Enter it EXACTLY the same way, even if any of the information is missing or incorrect. Fill in the corresponding ovals. If you do not complete these blocks to match your previous information EXACTLY, your scores will be **delayed up to 8 weeks**.

ACT®
PO BOX 168, IOWA CITY, IA 52243-0168

B MATCH NAME
(First 5 letters of last name)

A B C D E F G H I J K L M N O P Q R S T U V W X Y Z

C MATCH NUMBER

1 2 3 4 5 6 7 8 9 0

D DATE OF BIRTH

Month	Day	Year
January		
February		
March	1	1
April	2	2
May	3	3
June	4	
July	5	
August	6	
September	7	
October	8	
November	9	
December	0	

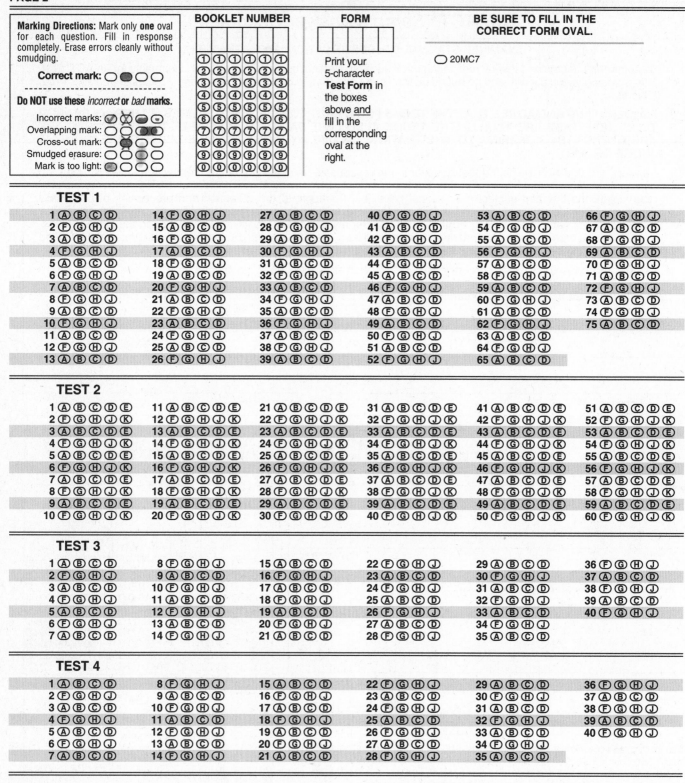

Marking Directions: Mark only **one** oval for each question. Fill in response completely. Erase errors cleanly without smudging.

Correct mark: ○ ● ○ ○

Do NOT use these *incorrect* or *bad* **marks.**

Incorrect marks: ⊘ ⊗ ◖ ⊙
Overlapping mark: ○○ ◕◖
Cross-out mark: ○○ ◕○
Smudged erasure: ○○ ◕○
Mark is too light: ◔ ○○ ○

BOOKLET NUMBER

FORM

Print your 5-character **Test Form** in the boxes above <u>and</u> fill in the corresponding oval at the right.

BE SURE TO FILL IN THE CORRECT FORM OVAL.

○ 20MC7

TEST 1

1 Ⓐ Ⓑ Ⓒ Ⓓ	14 Ⓕ Ⓖ Ⓗ Ⓙ	27 Ⓐ Ⓑ Ⓒ Ⓓ	40 Ⓕ Ⓖ Ⓗ Ⓙ	53 Ⓐ Ⓑ Ⓒ Ⓓ	66 Ⓕ Ⓖ Ⓗ Ⓙ
2 Ⓕ Ⓖ Ⓗ Ⓙ	15 Ⓐ Ⓑ Ⓒ Ⓓ	28 Ⓕ Ⓖ Ⓗ Ⓙ	41 Ⓐ Ⓑ Ⓒ Ⓓ	54 Ⓕ Ⓖ Ⓗ Ⓙ	67 Ⓐ Ⓑ Ⓒ Ⓓ
3 Ⓐ Ⓑ Ⓒ Ⓓ	16 Ⓕ Ⓖ Ⓗ Ⓙ	29 Ⓐ Ⓑ Ⓒ Ⓓ	42 Ⓕ Ⓖ Ⓗ Ⓙ	55 Ⓐ Ⓑ Ⓒ Ⓓ	68 Ⓕ Ⓖ Ⓗ Ⓙ
4 Ⓕ Ⓖ Ⓗ Ⓙ	17 Ⓐ Ⓑ Ⓒ Ⓓ	30 Ⓕ Ⓖ Ⓗ Ⓙ	43 Ⓐ Ⓑ Ⓒ Ⓓ	56 Ⓕ Ⓖ Ⓗ Ⓙ	69 Ⓐ Ⓑ Ⓒ Ⓓ
5 Ⓐ Ⓑ Ⓒ Ⓓ	18 Ⓕ Ⓖ Ⓗ Ⓙ	31 Ⓐ Ⓑ Ⓒ Ⓓ	44 Ⓕ Ⓖ Ⓗ Ⓙ	57 Ⓐ Ⓑ Ⓒ Ⓓ	70 Ⓕ Ⓖ Ⓗ Ⓙ
6 Ⓕ Ⓖ Ⓗ Ⓙ	19 Ⓐ Ⓑ Ⓒ Ⓓ	32 Ⓕ Ⓖ Ⓗ Ⓙ	45 Ⓐ Ⓑ Ⓒ Ⓓ	58 Ⓕ Ⓖ Ⓗ Ⓙ	71 Ⓐ Ⓑ Ⓒ Ⓓ
7 Ⓐ Ⓑ Ⓒ Ⓓ	20 Ⓕ Ⓖ Ⓗ Ⓙ	33 Ⓐ Ⓑ Ⓒ Ⓓ	46 Ⓕ Ⓖ Ⓗ Ⓙ	59 Ⓐ Ⓑ Ⓒ Ⓓ	72 Ⓕ Ⓖ Ⓗ Ⓙ
8 Ⓕ Ⓖ Ⓗ Ⓙ	21 Ⓐ Ⓑ Ⓒ Ⓓ	34 Ⓕ Ⓖ Ⓗ Ⓙ	47 Ⓐ Ⓑ Ⓒ Ⓓ	60 Ⓕ Ⓖ Ⓗ Ⓙ	73 Ⓐ Ⓑ Ⓒ Ⓓ
9 Ⓐ Ⓑ Ⓒ Ⓓ	22 Ⓕ Ⓖ Ⓗ Ⓙ	35 Ⓐ Ⓑ Ⓒ Ⓓ	48 Ⓕ Ⓖ Ⓗ Ⓙ	61 Ⓐ Ⓑ Ⓒ Ⓓ	74 Ⓕ Ⓖ Ⓗ Ⓙ
10 Ⓕ Ⓖ Ⓗ Ⓙ	23 Ⓐ Ⓑ Ⓒ Ⓓ	36 Ⓕ Ⓖ Ⓗ Ⓙ	49 Ⓐ Ⓑ Ⓒ Ⓓ	62 Ⓕ Ⓖ Ⓗ Ⓙ	75 Ⓐ Ⓑ Ⓒ Ⓓ
11 Ⓐ Ⓑ Ⓒ Ⓓ	24 Ⓕ Ⓖ Ⓗ Ⓙ	37 Ⓐ Ⓑ Ⓒ Ⓓ	50 Ⓕ Ⓖ Ⓗ Ⓙ	63 Ⓐ Ⓑ Ⓒ Ⓓ	
12 Ⓕ Ⓖ Ⓗ Ⓙ	25 Ⓐ Ⓑ Ⓒ Ⓓ	38 Ⓕ Ⓖ Ⓗ Ⓙ	51 Ⓐ Ⓑ Ⓒ Ⓓ	64 Ⓕ Ⓖ Ⓗ Ⓙ	
13 Ⓐ Ⓑ Ⓒ Ⓓ	26 Ⓕ Ⓖ Ⓗ Ⓙ	39 Ⓐ Ⓑ Ⓒ Ⓓ	52 Ⓕ Ⓖ Ⓗ Ⓙ	65 Ⓐ Ⓑ Ⓒ Ⓓ	

TEST 2

1 Ⓐ Ⓑ Ⓒ Ⓓ Ⓔ	11 Ⓐ Ⓑ Ⓒ Ⓓ Ⓔ	21 Ⓐ Ⓑ Ⓒ Ⓓ Ⓔ	31 Ⓐ Ⓑ Ⓒ Ⓓ Ⓔ	41 Ⓐ Ⓑ Ⓒ Ⓓ Ⓔ	51 Ⓐ Ⓑ Ⓒ Ⓓ Ⓔ
2 Ⓕ Ⓖ Ⓗ Ⓙ Ⓚ	12 Ⓕ Ⓖ Ⓗ Ⓙ Ⓚ	22 Ⓕ Ⓖ Ⓗ Ⓙ Ⓚ	32 Ⓕ Ⓖ Ⓗ Ⓙ Ⓚ	42 Ⓕ Ⓖ Ⓗ Ⓙ Ⓚ	52 Ⓕ Ⓖ Ⓗ Ⓙ Ⓚ
3 Ⓐ Ⓑ Ⓒ Ⓓ Ⓔ	13 Ⓐ Ⓑ Ⓒ Ⓓ Ⓔ	23 Ⓐ Ⓑ Ⓒ Ⓓ Ⓔ	33 Ⓐ Ⓑ Ⓒ Ⓓ Ⓔ	43 Ⓐ Ⓑ Ⓒ Ⓓ Ⓔ	53 Ⓐ Ⓑ Ⓒ Ⓓ Ⓔ
4 Ⓕ Ⓖ Ⓗ Ⓙ Ⓚ	14 Ⓕ Ⓖ Ⓗ Ⓙ Ⓚ	24 Ⓕ Ⓖ Ⓗ Ⓙ Ⓚ	34 Ⓕ Ⓖ Ⓗ Ⓙ Ⓚ	44 Ⓕ Ⓖ Ⓗ Ⓙ Ⓚ	54 Ⓕ Ⓖ Ⓗ Ⓙ Ⓚ
5 Ⓐ Ⓑ Ⓒ Ⓓ Ⓔ	15 Ⓐ Ⓑ Ⓒ Ⓓ Ⓔ	25 Ⓐ Ⓑ Ⓒ Ⓓ Ⓔ	35 Ⓐ Ⓑ Ⓒ Ⓓ Ⓔ	45 Ⓐ Ⓑ Ⓒ Ⓓ Ⓔ	55 Ⓐ Ⓑ Ⓒ Ⓓ Ⓔ
6 Ⓕ Ⓖ Ⓗ Ⓙ Ⓚ	16 Ⓕ Ⓖ Ⓗ Ⓙ Ⓚ	26 Ⓕ Ⓖ Ⓗ Ⓙ Ⓚ	36 Ⓕ Ⓖ Ⓗ Ⓙ Ⓚ	46 Ⓕ Ⓖ Ⓗ Ⓙ Ⓚ	56 Ⓕ Ⓖ Ⓗ Ⓙ Ⓚ
7 Ⓐ Ⓑ Ⓒ Ⓓ Ⓔ	17 Ⓐ Ⓑ Ⓒ Ⓓ Ⓔ	27 Ⓐ Ⓑ Ⓒ Ⓓ Ⓔ	37 Ⓐ Ⓑ Ⓒ Ⓓ Ⓔ	47 Ⓐ Ⓑ Ⓒ Ⓓ Ⓔ	57 Ⓐ Ⓑ Ⓒ Ⓓ Ⓔ
8 Ⓕ Ⓖ Ⓗ Ⓙ Ⓚ	18 Ⓕ Ⓖ Ⓗ Ⓙ Ⓚ	28 Ⓕ Ⓖ Ⓗ Ⓙ Ⓚ	38 Ⓕ Ⓖ Ⓗ Ⓙ Ⓚ	48 Ⓕ Ⓖ Ⓗ Ⓙ Ⓚ	58 Ⓕ Ⓖ Ⓗ Ⓙ Ⓚ
9 Ⓐ Ⓑ Ⓒ Ⓓ Ⓔ	19 Ⓐ Ⓑ Ⓒ Ⓓ Ⓔ	29 Ⓐ Ⓑ Ⓒ Ⓓ Ⓔ	39 Ⓐ Ⓑ Ⓒ Ⓓ Ⓔ	49 Ⓐ Ⓑ Ⓒ Ⓓ Ⓔ	59 Ⓐ Ⓑ Ⓒ Ⓓ Ⓔ
10 Ⓕ Ⓖ Ⓗ Ⓙ Ⓚ	20 Ⓕ Ⓖ Ⓗ Ⓙ Ⓚ	30 Ⓕ Ⓖ Ⓗ Ⓙ Ⓚ	40 Ⓕ Ⓖ Ⓗ Ⓙ Ⓚ	50 Ⓕ Ⓖ Ⓗ Ⓙ Ⓚ	60 Ⓕ Ⓖ Ⓗ Ⓙ Ⓚ

TEST 3

1 Ⓐ Ⓑ Ⓒ Ⓓ	8 Ⓕ Ⓖ Ⓗ Ⓙ	15 Ⓐ Ⓑ Ⓒ Ⓓ	22 Ⓕ Ⓖ Ⓗ Ⓙ	29 Ⓐ Ⓑ Ⓒ Ⓓ	36 Ⓕ Ⓖ Ⓗ Ⓙ
2 Ⓕ Ⓖ Ⓗ Ⓙ	9 Ⓐ Ⓑ Ⓒ Ⓓ	16 Ⓕ Ⓖ Ⓗ Ⓙ	23 Ⓐ Ⓑ Ⓒ Ⓓ	30 Ⓕ Ⓖ Ⓗ Ⓙ	37 Ⓐ Ⓑ Ⓒ Ⓓ
3 Ⓐ Ⓑ Ⓒ Ⓓ	10 Ⓕ Ⓖ Ⓗ Ⓙ	17 Ⓐ Ⓑ Ⓒ Ⓓ	24 Ⓕ Ⓖ Ⓗ Ⓙ	31 Ⓐ Ⓑ Ⓒ Ⓓ	38 Ⓕ Ⓖ Ⓗ Ⓙ
4 Ⓕ Ⓖ Ⓗ Ⓙ	11 Ⓐ Ⓑ Ⓒ Ⓓ	18 Ⓕ Ⓖ Ⓗ Ⓙ	25 Ⓐ Ⓑ Ⓒ Ⓓ	32 Ⓕ Ⓖ Ⓗ Ⓙ	39 Ⓐ Ⓑ Ⓒ Ⓓ
5 Ⓐ Ⓑ Ⓒ Ⓓ	12 Ⓕ Ⓖ Ⓗ Ⓙ	19 Ⓐ Ⓑ Ⓒ Ⓓ	26 Ⓕ Ⓖ Ⓗ Ⓙ	33 Ⓐ Ⓑ Ⓒ Ⓓ	40 Ⓕ Ⓖ Ⓗ Ⓙ
6 Ⓕ Ⓖ Ⓗ Ⓙ	13 Ⓐ Ⓑ Ⓒ Ⓓ	20 Ⓕ Ⓖ Ⓗ Ⓙ	27 Ⓐ Ⓑ Ⓒ Ⓓ	34 Ⓕ Ⓖ Ⓗ Ⓙ	
7 Ⓐ Ⓑ Ⓒ Ⓓ	14 Ⓕ Ⓖ Ⓗ Ⓙ	21 Ⓐ Ⓑ Ⓒ Ⓓ	28 Ⓕ Ⓖ Ⓗ Ⓙ	35 Ⓐ Ⓑ Ⓒ Ⓓ	

TEST 4

1 Ⓐ Ⓑ Ⓒ Ⓓ	8 Ⓕ Ⓖ Ⓗ Ⓙ	15 Ⓐ Ⓑ Ⓒ Ⓓ	22 Ⓕ Ⓖ Ⓗ Ⓙ	29 Ⓐ Ⓑ Ⓒ Ⓓ	36 Ⓕ Ⓖ Ⓗ Ⓙ
2 Ⓕ Ⓖ Ⓗ Ⓙ	9 Ⓐ Ⓑ Ⓒ Ⓓ	16 Ⓕ Ⓖ Ⓗ Ⓙ	23 Ⓐ Ⓑ Ⓒ Ⓓ	30 Ⓕ Ⓖ Ⓗ Ⓙ	37 Ⓐ Ⓑ Ⓒ Ⓓ
3 Ⓐ Ⓑ Ⓒ Ⓓ	10 Ⓕ Ⓖ Ⓗ Ⓙ	17 Ⓐ Ⓑ Ⓒ Ⓓ	24 Ⓕ Ⓖ Ⓗ Ⓙ	31 Ⓐ Ⓑ Ⓒ Ⓓ	38 Ⓕ Ⓖ Ⓗ Ⓙ
4 Ⓕ Ⓖ Ⓗ Ⓙ	11 Ⓐ Ⓑ Ⓒ Ⓓ	18 Ⓕ Ⓖ Ⓗ Ⓙ	25 Ⓐ Ⓑ Ⓒ Ⓓ	32 Ⓕ Ⓖ Ⓗ Ⓙ	39 Ⓐ Ⓑ Ⓒ Ⓓ
5 Ⓐ Ⓑ Ⓒ Ⓓ	12 Ⓕ Ⓖ Ⓗ Ⓙ	19 Ⓐ Ⓑ Ⓒ Ⓓ	26 Ⓕ Ⓖ Ⓗ Ⓙ	33 Ⓐ Ⓑ Ⓒ Ⓓ	40 Ⓕ Ⓖ Ⓗ Ⓙ
6 Ⓕ Ⓖ Ⓗ Ⓙ	13 Ⓐ Ⓑ Ⓒ Ⓓ	20 Ⓕ Ⓖ Ⓗ Ⓙ	27 Ⓐ Ⓑ Ⓒ Ⓓ	34 Ⓕ Ⓖ Ⓗ Ⓙ	
7 Ⓐ Ⓑ Ⓒ Ⓓ	14 Ⓕ Ⓖ Ⓗ Ⓙ	21 Ⓐ Ⓑ Ⓒ Ⓓ	28 Ⓕ Ⓖ Ⓗ Ⓙ	35 Ⓐ Ⓑ Ⓒ Ⓓ	

190760

Practice Test

EXAMINEE STATEMENTS, CERTIFICATION, AND SIGNATURE

1. Statements: I understand that by registering for, launching, starting, or submitting answer documents for an ACT® test, I am agreeing to comply with and be bound by the *Terms and Conditions: Testing Rules and Policies for the ACT® Test* ("Terms").

I UNDERSTAND AND AGREE THAT THE TERMS PERMIT ACT TO CANCEL MY SCORES IF THERE IS REASON TO BELIEVE THEY ARE INVALID. THE TERMS ALSO LIMIT DAMAGES AVAILABLE TO ME AND REQUIRE ARBITRATION. BY AGREEING TO ARBITRATION, I WAIVE MY RIGHT TO HAVE DISPUTES HEARD BY A JUDGE OR JURY.

I understand that ACT owns the test questions and responses, and I will not share them with anyone by any form of communication before, during, or after the test administration. I understand that taking the test for someone else may violate the law and subject me to legal penalties. I consent to the collection and processing of personally identifying information I provide, and its subsequent use and disclosure, as described in the ACT Privacy Policy (www.act.org/privacy.html). I also permit ACT to transfer my personally identifying information to the United States, to ACT, or to a third-party service provider, where it will be subject to use and disclosure under the laws of the United States, including being accessible to law enforcement or national security authorities.

2. Certification: Copy the italicized certification below, then sign, date, and print your name in the spaces provided.

*I agree to the **Statements** above and certify that I am the person whose information appears on this form.*

_____

_____

_____   _____   _____
Your Signature   Today's Date   Print Your Name

 **Form 20MC7**

2019 | 2020

Directions

This booklet contains tests in English, mathematics, reading, and science. These tests measure skills and abilities highly related to high school course work and success in college. **Calculators may be used on the mathematics test only.**

The questions in each test are numbered, and the suggested answers for each question are lettered. On the answer document, the rows of ovals are numbered to match the questions, and the ovals in each row are lettered to correspond to the suggested answers.

For each question, first decide which answer is best. Next, locate on the answer document the row of ovals numbered the same as the question. Then, locate the oval in that row lettered the same as your answer. Finally, fill in the oval completely. Use a soft lead pencil and make your marks heavy and black. **Do not use ink or a mechanical pencil.**

Mark only one answer to each question. If you change your mind about an answer, erase your first mark thoroughly before marking your new answer. For each question, make certain that you mark in the row of ovals with the same number as the question.

Only responses marked on your answer document will be scored. Your score on each test will be based only on the number of questions you answer correctly during the time allowed for that test. You will **not** be penalized for guessing. **It is to your advantage to answer every question even if you must guess.**

You may work on each test **only** when the testing staff tells you to do so. If you finish a test before time is called for that test, you should use the time remaining to reconsider questions you are uncertain about in that test. You may **not** look back to a test on which time has already been called, and you may **not** go ahead to another test. To do so will disqualify you from the examination.

Lay your pencil down immediately when time is called at the end of each test. You may **not** for any reason fill in or alter ovals for a test after time is called for that test. To do so will disqualify you from the examination.

Do not fold or tear the pages of your test booklet.

**DO NOT OPEN THIS BOOKLET
UNTIL TOLD TO DO SO.**

1 ■ ■ ■ ■ ■ ■ ■ ■ ■ 1

ENGLISH TEST
45 Minutes—75 Questions

DIRECTIONS: In the five passages that follow, certain words and phrases are underlined and numbered. In the right-hand column, you will find alternatives for the underlined part. In most cases, you are to choose the one that best expresses the idea, makes the statement appropriate for standard written English, or is worded most consistently with the style and tone of the passage as a whole. If you think the original version is best, choose "NO CHANGE." In some cases, you will find in the right-hand column a question about the underlined part. You are to choose the best answer to the question.

You will also find questions about a section of the passage, or about the passage as a whole. These questions do not refer to an underlined portion of the passage, but rather are identified by a number or numbers in a box.

For each question, choose the alternative you consider best and fill in the corresponding oval on your answer document. Read each passage through once before you begin to answer the questions that accompany it. For many of the questions, you must read several sentences beyond the question to determine the answer. Be sure that you have read far enough ahead each time you choose an alternative.

PASSAGE I

Albino Redwoods

At Henry Cowell State Park in Felton, California, a waxy white bush leans against the majestic trunk of a 500-year-old, 20-story-tall coastal redwood tree. The bush is distinctive, it has an unusual incandescence and only
[1]
stands about four feet tall. Surprisingly, though, the bush is almost genetically identical to the enormous redwood that dwarfs it. The bush—a rare botanical anomaly—is
[2]
an albino coastal redwood.

1. **A.** NO CHANGE
   B. distinctive, it has an unusual incandescence,
   C. distinctive; it has an unusual incandescence
   D. distinctive it has an unusual incandescence

2. **F.** NO CHANGE
   G. bush a rare botanical anomaly—
   H. bush, a rare botanical anomaly—
   J. bush—a rare botanical anomaly

GO ON TO THE NEXT PAGE.

1 ■ ■ ■ ■ ■ ■ ■ ■ ■ 1

These exceptional shrubs lack the most essential plant characteristic: the ability to produce chlorophyll, which absorbs light most strongly in the blue portion of the electromagnetic spectrum. ⬛3 Without chlorophyll, photosynthesis cannot occur, leaving albino coastal

redwoods without a means of producing <u>its</u> own food.
4

<u>Contrastingly,</u> in order to survive, these plants become
5

<u>parasites. Latching</u> onto the roots of nearby redwoods
6
to tap into their nutrients. During periods of drought,

albino redwoods often wither and <u>enter</u> a dormant
7
state. Later, during periods of heavy rainfall, they

<u>resurrect back to life and latch</u> onto their hosts.
8

3. The writer is considering deleting the following clause from the preceding sentence (adjusting the punctuation as needed):

> which absorbs light most strongly in the blue portion of the electromagnetic spectrum

Given that the information is accurate, should the writer make this deletion?

A. Yes, because the information is implied by information in the previous paragraph.
B. Yes, because the information is irrelevant to the scope and focus of the paragraph.
C. No, because the information clarifies how albino coastal redwoods can survive without producing chlorophyll.
D. No, because the information clarifies why coastal redwood trees can grow to such astounding heights.

4. F. NO CHANGE
   G. their
   H. it's
   J. its'

5. A. NO CHANGE
   B. Accordingly,
   C. Similarly,
   D. Besides,

6. F. NO CHANGE
   G. parasites and latching
   H. parasites, latching
   J. parasites; latching

7. A. NO CHANGE
   B. introduce
   C. invade
   D. access

8. F. NO CHANGE
   G. resurrect in reanimation to latch
   H. revive to life again, latching
   J. revive and latch back

GO ON TO THE NEXT PAGE.

1   **1**

Although these plants may seem like little more
                                    9
than botanical leeches, they are actually a testament
        9

from the tree's remarkable genetics and adaptability.
    10
Coastal redwoods have six pairs of chromosomes. This

allows them an extraordinary degree of genetic diversity.

Every time a new coastal redwood sprouts, an abundance

of possible genetic mutations can occur. Most of these

mutations benefit the tree, such as making it more resistant

to fungi or viruses. But on occasion an albino mutation

of the forest can occur, creating this rare phenomenon.
    11

Botanists appraise there are only about sixty albino
            12
coastal redwoods in the world. Geneticists are now

thinking more or less about the chromosomal makeup
        13
of these rare specimens. While scientists are still

baffled by what function albino coastal redwoods

serve in forests. Conservationists continue to advocate
        14
for their preservation. At the very least, albino coastal

redwoods are not only a rare phenomenon but also a

stunning illumination in the diversity found in the
                            15
natural world.

9. Given that all the choices are accurate, which one most
   effectively leads the reader from the preceding para-
   graph to the new paragraph?
   A. NO CHANGE
   B. Although these plants have been found in the
      forests of Northern California,
   C. While park rangers have made concerted efforts to
      protect these plants,
   D. While these plants are not nearly as tall as other
      coastal redwoods,

10. F. NO CHANGE
    G. since
    H. to
    J. in

11. The best placement for the underlined portion would
    be:
    A. where it is now.
    B. after the word *occasion*.
    C. after the word *creating*.
    D. after the word *phenomenon* (and before the
       period).

12. F. NO CHANGE
    G. interpret
    H. estimate
    J. foresee

13. The writer wants to emphasize that geneticists are now
    researching the genetic makeup of albino coastal red-
    woods more thoroughly. Which choice best accom-
    plishes that goal?
    A. NO CHANGE
    B. delving deeper into
    C. looking haphazardly at
    D. intermittently exploring

14. F. NO CHANGE
    G. forests, and conservationists
    H. forests and conservationists
    J. forests, conservationists

15. A. NO CHANGE
    B. of the diversity found of
    C. of the diversity found in
    D. in the diversity found of

GO ON TO THE NEXT PAGE.

1 ▪ ▪ ▪ ▪ ▪ ▪ ▪ ▪ 1

PASSAGE II

Diving the Bonne Terre Mine

In 1962, one of the main producers of lead in the United States for almost a century, the Bonne Terre Mine in Bonne Terre, Missouri, was shut down due to falling profits. With equipment and <u>tools still deep within the mine,</u> the entrance was
₁₆
boarded up, the pumps that had kept the mine dry for decades turned off. ▢17 Now, the site is visited by

thousands of scuba divers every year, those <u>who looked</u>
₁₈

for an unusual dive in what <u>sometimes is considered as like</u>
₁₉
an underwater mining museum.

The abandoned mine is shaped like a giant cone, with each of its five levels becoming successively narrower. A series of chutes, passageways, and ore dumps connects the levels. Sprawling beneath the four-square-mile town of Bonne Terre, <u>however,</u> the mine contains
₂₀

over eighty square miles of <u>larger-than-life</u>
₂₁
rooms and at least seventeen miles of tunnels.

16. F. NO CHANGE
    G. tools (still deep within the mine)
    H. tools, still deep within the mine,
    J. tools, still deep within the mine

17. Which of the following true statements, if added here, would provide the best transition between the account of the mine's history and the description of its current use?
    A. The original 946 acres of land of the Bonne Terre Mine site were purchased in 1864 by the St. Joseph Lead Company.
    B. Groundwater began to seep in, eventually filling most of the mine and forming one of the world's largest underground lakes.
    C. Visitors not interested in scuba diving are welcome to take walking tours or boat tours of the upper levels of the mine.
    D. The views of the mine from underwater are breathtaking—the mine is both a natural and a human-made wonder.

18. F. NO CHANGE
    G. who were to look
    H. are to look
    J. looking

19. A. NO CHANGE
    B. is labeled as it may as
    C. might be called
    D. seems as

20. F. NO CHANGE
    G. for example,
    H. therefore,
    J. DELETE the underlined portion.

21. Which choice emphasizes the large size of the rooms of the mine with the clearest and most specific reference to scale?
    A. NO CHANGE
    B. stadium-sized
    C. unbelievable
    D. expansive

GO ON TO THE NEXT PAGE.

1 ■ ■ ■ ■   ■ ■ ■ ■ **1**

The cool water that fills the mine that is below the
city of Bonne Terre is remarkably clean and clear.

[1] Divers enter the mine through a small outbuilding in Bonne Terre. [2] At the very bottom of the mine still stands the timekeeper's shack, where workers clocked in at the beginning of a shift. [3] Inside, 500,000-watt floodlights gleam the dry top level of the mine, where walking tours are held. [4] The main diving docks are about a quarter mile within the mine, on the second level. [5] On guided tours, divers explore tunnels filled with ore carts, rock drills, dynamite boxes, and other artifacts from the mine's possession. [6] Smooth walls and ceilings

stretch for miles, and shimmer with deposits of cobalt,

copper, calcium, and iron; pillars of unexcavated rock support the ceilings. [7] Near the shack, a rusting

locomotive lies on its side. 28

The site was explored by
internationally renowned French diver
Jacques Cousteau and has been featured in many travel and adventure publications. Divers from around the world visit the Bonne Terre Mine site keep swimming into a fascinating past.

---

22. F. NO CHANGE
G. this sprawling, cone-shaped mine
H. this mine with five levels
J. the mine

23. A. NO CHANGE
B. shack, there
C. shack; where
D. shack,

24. F. NO CHANGE
G. illuminate
H. radiate
J. enlighten

25. A. NO CHANGE
B. the working days of the mine.
C. when it worked.
D. then.

26. F. NO CHANGE
G. miles and shimmer
H. miles, and shimmer,
J. miles and shimmer,

27. Which of the following alternatives to the underlined portion would NOT be acceptable?
A. iron; throughout the mine, pillars
B. iron, while pillars
C. iron, pillars
D. iron. Pillars

28. For the sake of the logic and coherence of this paragraph, Sentence 2 should be placed:
F. where it is now.
G. after Sentence 3.
H. after Sentence 4.
J. after Sentence 6.

29. Given that all the choices are accurate, which one provides the clearest and most relevant information at this point in the essay?
A. NO CHANGE
B. someone many people have heard of named
C. winner of awards in several areas
D. tourist and Frenchman

30. F. NO CHANGE
G. as it swims
H. that swims
J. to swim

GO ON TO THE NEXT PAGE.

1 ▪ ▪ ▪ ▪ ▪ ▪ ▪ ▪ ▪ ▪ 1

PASSAGE III

Pitch Perfect

Even at age seven, Mozart presented
₃₁
audiences with his musical talents, including

the ability to identify accurately any note he heard.

This aptitude, recognizing notes without aid—is called
₃₂

absolute pitch. People with absolute pitch usually
₃₃
possess related musical skills, such as being able to

sing any requested note perfectly.

For decades, the fraction sited in scientific
₃₄
literature has been that only one person per ten

thousand has absolute pitch. Such rarity renders

absolute pitch so wicked sweet to scientists, many of
₃₅
whom have long suspected that the ability has a genetic

basis. Absolute pitch appears to run in families, after all.

And in 2009 a team led by geneticist Jane Gitschier found

positive correlation between specific chromosomes and

absolute pitch.

On the other hand, psychologist Diana

Deutsch, in arguing that language is key to
₃₆
a person's chances of having absolute pitch.

Deutsch found that people fluent in "tone

languages"—such as Mandarin, where a word

conveys different meanings depending on the

pitch in which it is spoken—were much more

likely to have absolute pitch than speakers of English

and other nontone languages. One of Deutsch's

studies paraded that more than 90 percent of music
₃₇
students fluent in a tone language had absolute pitch.

31. Which choice most clearly indicates the audiences' reaction to young Mozart's musical talents?
   A. NO CHANGE
   B. aimed to entertain
   C. appeared before
   D. dazzled

32. F. NO CHANGE
   G. aptitude—recognizing notes without aid—
   H. aptitude—recognizing notes without aid,
   J. aptitude, recognizing notes without aid

33. A. NO CHANGE
   B. pitch and those people
   C. pitch and people
   D. pitch, people

34. F. NO CHANGE
   G. numeral sited
   H. figure cited
   J. digit cited

35. A. NO CHANGE
   B. a problematic phenomenon that presents a captivating conundrum
   C. all the more fascinating
   D. totally nifty

36. F. NO CHANGE
   G. Deutsch argues
   H. Deutsch. She argues
   J. Deutsch, who argues

37. A. NO CHANGE
   B. broadcast
   C. showed
   D. bared

GO ON TO THE NEXT PAGE.

1 ■ ■ ■ ■ ■ ■ ■ ■ ■ **1**

Clearly, that's dramatically higher than the
       ——————
        38

previously mentioned statistic of one person
——————————
        39
per ten thousand.

Deutsch suggests that children learning tone
        ————————————————————————
                              40
languages develop the ability to associate pitch with
————————
   40
meaning, which is analogous to someone with absolute

pitch associating a pitch with the name of the note.

In early childhood, as the brain goes through a phase

of development during which it is primed to learn

language, which can likewise be able to learn
          ———————
            41

absolute pitch. [42] If a child is studying music

during this particular period, that further increases

his or her chances of developing absolute pitch.

As for the dismal chances of learning absolute pitch
————————————————————————————————————
                         43

as an adult, the odds aren't good: there has never
                              ————
                               44
been a proven case of success.

38. F. NO CHANGE
    G. With this in mind,
    H. As a result,
    J. Besides,

39. Given that all the choices are accurate, which one most clearly suggests that the ideas about the prevalence of absolute pitch are changing?

    A. NO CHANGE
    B. often referred to
    C. once-accepted
    D. infinitesimal

40. F. NO CHANGE
    G. suggests, that children learning tone languages,
    H. suggests that children, learning tone languages,
    J. suggests, that children learning tone languages

41. A. NO CHANGE
    B. the brain may
    C. to
    D. DELETE the underlined portion.

42. At this point, the writer is considering dividing the paragraph into two. Should the writer begin or not begin a new paragraph here, and why?

    F. Begin a new paragraph, because the essay shifts at this point from focusing on children and absolute pitch to focusing on adults and absolute pitch.
    G. Begin a new paragraph, because it would separate the ideas about language development and absolute pitch from the essay's conclusion.
    H. DO NOT begin a new paragraph, because doing so would establish a link between early childhood music education and absolute pitch.
    J. DO NOT begin a new paragraph, because doing so would interrupt the discussion of childhood influences on absolute pitch.

43. A. NO CHANGE
    B. learning absolute pitch so that it is something you have acquired
    C. a grown-up learning absolute pitch
    D. acquiring absolute pitch

44. F. NO CHANGE
    G. good; and
    H. good,
    J. good

GO ON TO THE NEXT PAGE.

1 ■ ■ ■ ■ ■ ■ ■ ■ ■ 1

Question 45 asks about the preceding passage as a whole.

---

45. Suppose the writer's primary purpose had been to equally consider Gitschier's and Deutsch's theories regarding the reasons some people develop absolute pitch. Would this essay accomplish that purpose?

   A. Yes, because it considers both of the theories with equivalent depth and breadth.

   B. Yes, because it clearly outlines the reasons why Gitschier's theory is the correct one.

   C. No, because it explores Deutsch's theory more thoroughly than it does Gitschier's.

   D. No, because it displays a bias against Deutsch's theory, preventing a balanced comparison.

PASSAGE IV

George Masa and the Smoky Mountains

Masa Knob, a densely <u>forested peek</u> in Great Smoky
₄₆

Mountains National Park, isn't <u>as majestic a</u> park attraction
₄₇

as Clingmans Dome or Laurel Falls. It's a humble

landmark named <u>for</u> a man who tirelessly explored,
₄₈

documented, and fought to <u>protect and</u> would become
₄₉

the most visited national park in the United States.

Japanese <u>immigrant, Iizuka Masahara,</u> adopted
₅₀

the name George Masa in 1915, when he took a job as a

bellman at an upscale hotel in Asheville, North Carolina.

He often took pictures of hotel guests. Masa's photos

depict prosperous <u>vacations,</u> some enjoying hikes
₅₁

organized by Masa himself. Three years after

settling in Asheville, <u>which was when</u> Masa
₅₂

opened a photography studio.

---

46. **F.** NO CHANGE
   G. forested peak
   H. forest peak
   J. forest peek

47. **A.** NO CHANGE
   B. so much a majestic
   C. as majestic as the
   D. majestically a

48. **F.** NO CHANGE
   G. from
   H. upon
   J. of

49. **A.** NO CHANGE
   B. protect it, which
   C. protect, which
   D. protect what

50. **F.** NO CHANGE
   G. immigrant, Iizuka Masahara
   H. immigrant Iizuka Masahara,
   J. immigrant Iizuka Masahara

51. **A.** NO CHANGE
   B. vacationers,
   C. vacation scenes,
   D. vacationing,

52. **F.** NO CHANGE
   G. it was then that
   H. at which point
   J. DELETE the underlined portion.

GO ON TO THE NEXT PAGE.

1 ▪ ▪ ▪ ▪ ▪ ▪ ▪ ▪ 1

The fog-shrouded mountains surrounding Asheville frequently lured Masa, with heavy, unwieldy camera equipment in tow, out of the studio he'd opened in Asheville. Morning hikes became weeks-long expeditions. To get the perfect shot, Masa would scale the highest mountains, lugging his equipment on his back. He sometimes waited hours for the clouds to arrange themselves to his liking before he took a picture.

Masa's measuring instruments were innovative. Using an odometer mounted on the detached front end of a bicycle, Masa measured his routes. He pushed the contraption across the steep terrain, hiking and measuring, measuring and hiking, year after year. From these measurements, he produced detailed maps.

Masa made it his mission to ensure that the land he treasured would be preserved as a national park. He gave his photos and maps to prominent Asheville visitors, recruiting First Lady Grace Coolidge and wealthy philanthropist John D. Rockefeller Jr., among others, to join the park campaign. In reality, to build support from the wider public, Masa distributed thousands of postcards of his photos.

53. A. NO CHANGE
    B. his studio and into the mountains.
    C. his studio.
    D. there.

54. Which choice most effectively emphasizes that Masa's equipment was unwieldy?
    F. NO CHANGE
    G. transporting
    H. carrying
    J. taking

55. Given that all the statements are true, which one provides the most effective transition from the preceding paragraph to this paragraph?
    A. NO CHANGE
    B. Masa wasn't content only exploring and photographing the mountains, however.
    C. Masa's photos of the Smoky Mountains were not only detailed, but also artistic.
    D. Bicycling was another of Masa's interests.

56. F. NO CHANGE
    G. amid other big shots,
    H. and so forth,
    J. et cetera,

57. A. NO CHANGE
    B. All in all,
    C. Then,
    D. Thus,

1 ■ ■ ■ ■ ■ ■ ■ ■ ■ 1

Great Smoky Mountains National Park was established in 1934, a year after Masa's death. Although not many park visitors climb Masa Knob or know about it's namesake and advocate,
58

I think they should.
59

58. **F.** NO CHANGE
  G. they're
  H. their
  J. its

59. Which choice most effectively concludes the sentence and the essay?
  A. NO CHANGE
  B. archivists still search for Masa's photographs today.
  C. they all owe their visit in part to George Masa.
  D. it can be found just off the Appalachian Trail.

Question 60 asks about the preceding passage as a whole.

60. Suppose the writer's primary purpose had been to describe how an artist discovered and developed his or her talent. Would this essay accomplish that purpose?
  F. Yes, because the writer indicates that visitors to Asheville inspired Masa to try out photography.
  G. Yes, because the writer describes tools that Masa created to refine his photography techniques.
  H. No, because the writer focuses on how Masa used his talents to help explore and preserve a specific area.
  J. No, because the writer admits that not many visitors to Great Smoky Mountains National Park know about Masa.

PASSAGE V

Cozy Graffiti

In 2005, Houston shop owner Magda Sayeg knit a blue-and-pink cozy, or fitted cover, for the street-side door handle of her store. It was a slow day; Sayeg was bored. To her surprise, the seemingly out-of-place little cozy drew a lot of attention and often made people smile. Inspired by the effects, Sayeg knit a leg warmer for the
61
stop sign on the corner. This time, drivers actually pulled over for a closer look. Some people even took pictures of

61. Which of the following alternatives to the underlined portion would NOT be acceptable?
  A. Because Sayeg was inspired by the effects, she
  B. The effects, which were inspiring for Sayeg,
  C. Sayeg, taking inspiration from the effects,
  D. The effects were inspiring for Sayeg; she

GO ON TO THE NEXT PAGE.

1 ■ ■ ■ ■ ■ ■ ■ ■ ■ ■ 1

the sign. As Sayeg expanded her territory around Houston, her then-anonymous projects gained notoriety online and in newspapers, sparking similar endeavors by knitters and crocheters around the globe.

Adopting the utterances of graffiti, these yarn artists
                    ――――――
                        62
commonly refer to the act of covering something with

knitted or crocheted yarn such as "tagging." They take
                            ――――――
                               63
measurements of an object they wish to cover, stitch at home, and then quietly wrap the object during the night.

Rather, in the morning, a park full of trees wrapped in
――――――
   64
striped leg warmers welcomes joggers. Giant metal chain

links on a wharf appear covered in violet, green, white,
                        ――――――
                            65

blue. Sidewalk cracks being filled with skinny, knitted
            ――――――――
                66
ropes of magenta.

Some yarn graffiti artists mainly want to
                    ―――――――――――
                         67
surprise people, offering a bit of homey comfort

where we're least expected. Others, however,
      ――――
        68

aim for a more political message, they drape
                            ―――――――
                                69
cannons and tanks in colorful crocheted afghans.

62. **F.** NO CHANGE
     G. verbalizations
     H. language
     J. talk

63. **A.** NO CHANGE
     B. like
     C. as
     D. to

64. **F.** NO CHANGE
     G. Specifically, in
     H. Meanwhile, in
     J. In

65. The writer wants to emphasize the idea that wrapping an object in yarn has the effect of softening the object's appearance. Which choice best accomplishes that goal?
     A. NO CHANGE
     B. new with freshly knitted yarn in
     C. highlighted in vibrant colors of
     D. swaddled in fuzzy hues of

66. **F.** NO CHANGE
     G. cracks, which are
     H. cracks are
     J. cracks

67. **A.** NO CHANGE
     B. artists, by mainly wanting
     C. artists who mainly want
     D. artists, mainly wanting

68. **F.** NO CHANGE
     G. you're
     H. one's
     J. it's

69. **A.** NO CHANGE
     B. such yarn artists have draped
     C. draping
     D. they might drape

GO ON TO THE NEXT PAGE.

1 ▪ ▪ ▪ ▪ ▪ ▪ ▪ ▪ ▪ ▪ 1

In 2011, knitter Jessie Hemmons decided she'd
                    ‾‾‾‾‾‾‾‾‾‾‾‾‾‾‾‾‾‾‾‾‾‾
                              70

had enough of people snapping pictures of the bronze

statue of Rocky (a fictional boxer) in front of the

Philadelphia Museum of Art without ever going inside

the museum. She crafted a bright pink hoodie for the
    ‾‾‾‾‾‾‾
       71

muscular figure, who was played by Sylvester Stallone
         ‾‾
                              72

in the *Rocky* movies.
‾‾‾‾‾‾‾‾‾‾‾‾‾‾‾‾‾‾
       72

Although yarn tagging is a form of graffiti,

it's tolerated more often than other forms because
   ‾‾‾‾‾‾‾‾‾‾‾‾‾‾‾‾‾‾‾‾‾‾‾
             73

the yarn can be simply snipped off. This may be the

aspect that allows people to smile as they drop coins

into a cozy, purple parking meter and to consider the

artist's sweet—or edgy point.
        ‾‾‾‾‾‾‾‾‾‾‾‾‾‾‾
              74

70. F. NO CHANGE
   G. knitter—Jessie Hemmons—
   H. knitter, Jessie Hemmons,
   J. knitter Jessie Hemmons,

71. A. NO CHANGE
   B. museum that they are standing in front of.
   C. building, which features works of art.
   D. Philadelphia Museum of Art.

72. Given that all the choices are accurate, which one best supports the idea the writer is putting forth at this point in the essay?
   F. NO CHANGE
   G. figure, which stands at the bottom of the seventy-two steps leading up to the museum entrance.
   H. figure and carried a stepladder to the site so she could reach the statue.
   J. figure, adding an embroidered imperative: "GO SEE THE ART."

73. A. NO CHANGE
   B. its' tolerated more often then
   C. it's tolerated more often then
   D. its tolerated more often than

74. F. NO CHANGE
   G. sweet—or edgy—
   H. sweet, or edgy
   J. sweet or edgy,

Question 75 asks about the preceding passage as a whole.

---

75. Suppose the writer's primary purpose had been to offer an overview of a cultural phenomenon. Would this essay accomplish that purpose?

   A. Yes, because it describes the range of Sayeg's yarn graffiti projects from the door handle cozy to larger projects throughout Houston.
   B. Yes, because it briefly traces the development of yarn graffiti, offers examples, and discusses the variety of artists' intentions.
   C. No, because it explains what yarn graffiti is but suggests that few people are involved in it.
   D. No, because it focuses mainly on creating a profile of Sayeg as the first yarn graffiti artist.

END OF TEST 1

STOP! DO NOT TURN THE PAGE UNTIL TOLD TO DO SO.

2   **2**

MATHEMATICS TEST

60 Minutes—60 Questions

DIRECTIONS: Solve each problem, choose the correct answer, and then fill in the corresponding oval on your answer document.

Do not linger over problems that take too much time. Solve as many as you can; then return to the others in the time you have left for this test.

You are permitted to use a calculator on this test. You may use your calculator for any problems you choose, but some of the problems may best be done without using a calculator.

Note: Unless otherwise stated, all of the following should be assumed.

1. Illustrative figures are NOT necessarily drawn to scale.
2. Geometric figures lie in a plane.
3. The word *line* indicates a straight line.
4. The word *average* indicates arithmetic mean.

---

1. A line in the standard (x,y) coordinate plane passes through the points $(-2,-6)$ and $(5,3)$. The slope of the line:

   A. is positive.
   B. is zero.
   C. is negative.
   D. is undefined.
   E. cannot be determined from the given information.

2. What is the sum of the complex numbers $3 - 4i$ and $5 + 3i$?

   F.   7
   G. 27
   H. $-1 + 8i$
   J. $8 - i$
   K. $15 - 12i$

3. Last year at RT University, the ratio of the number of students accepted to the number of students applying for admission was 2 to 7. RT University accepted 630 students last year. How many students applied to RT University last year?

   A.   810
   B. 1,260
   C. 2,205
   D. 2,835
   E. 4,410

DO YOUR FIGURING HERE.

GO ON TO THE NEXT PAGE.

2 △ △ △ △ △ △ △ △ △ **2**

4. Three line segments intersect as shown in the figure below, forming angles with measures of 150°, 40°, and $x°$, respectively. What is the value of x ?

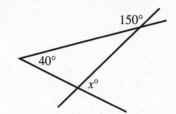

F. 95
G. 85
H. 80
J. 75
K. 70

DO YOUR FIGURING HERE.

5. A carnival game is played using an open box with a rectangular bottom measuring 6 inches by 13 inches. A square with side lengths of 4 inches is painted on the bottom of the box. The game is played by dropping a small bead into the open box. If the bead comes to rest in the painted square, the player wins a prize. Assuming a bead dropped into the box comes to rest at a random spot on the bottom of the box, which of the following is closest to the probability that the bead comes to rest in the painted square?

A. 0.05
B. 0.10
C. 0.21
D. 0.31
E. 0.67

6. What is the slope-intercept form of $9x - y - 5 = 0$?

F. $y = -9x - 5$
G. $y = -9x + 5$
H. $y = 9x - 5$
J. $y = 9x + 5$
K. $y = 5x - 9$

7. The line below contains X, Y, and Z, in that order. The ratio of the length of $\overline{XY}$ to the length of $\overline{YZ}$ is 5:9. If it can be determined, what is the ratio of the length of $\overline{XY}$ to the length of $\overline{XZ}$?

A. 5:14
B. 5:4
C. 9:5
D. 14:5
E. Cannot be determined from the given information

8. The solution set of $2x + 4 \geq -8$ is the set of all real values of x such that:

F. $x \geq -8$
G. $x \geq -6$
H. $x \leq -6$
J. $x \geq -2$
K. $x \leq -2$

GO ON TO THE NEXT PAGE.

2   **2**

9. Which of the following is equivalent to $\left(a^3\right)^{21}$?

   A. $63a$

   B. $24a$

   C. $3a^{21}$

   D. a^{24}

   E. a^{63}

DO YOUR FIGURING HERE.

10. If $f(x) = 3x^2 + 7x - 8$, then $f(-3) = ?$

    F. -47

    G. -2

    H. 2

    J. 40

    K. 52

11. Two sides of a triangle are equal in length. The third side is 3 centimeters longer than either of the other 2 sides. Given that the perimeter of the triangle is 93 centimeters, what is the length, in centimeters, of the longest side?

    A. 29

    B. 30

    C. 31

    D. 33

    E. 34

12. The 220 graduating seniors of Madison High School will sit in the center section of the school auditorium at the graduation ceremony. How many rows of seats will be needed to seat all of the graduating seniors if the first row has 10 seats and each succeeding row has 2 more seats than the previous row?

    F. 10

    G. 11

    H. 12

    J. 15

    K. 30

13. In the standard (x,y) coordinate plane, the point $(3,-7)$ is the midpoint of the line segment with endpoints $(9,-11)$ and:

    A. $(-3,-25)$

    B. $(-3, -3)$

    C. $(3, -2)$

    D. $(3, 3)$

    E. $(6, -9)$

GO ON TO THE NEXT PAGE.

2 △ △ △ △ △ △ △ △ △ 2

> Use the following information to answer questions 14–16.

A community theater group performed at 5 local schools. For each school, the table below shows the total number of tickets sold and the total dollar amount collected from ticket sales.

School	Number of tickets sold	Ticket sales
A	200	$1,400
B	250	$1,650
C	300	$1,800
D	150	$1,350
E	275	$1,625

14. At School A, only 2 types of tickets were sold: premium tickets for $10 each and value tickets for $6 each. How many value tickets were sold at School A ?

    F. 22
    G. 50
    H. 100
    J. 150
    K. 178

15. The theater group had to pay each school a facility charge. For use of its facility, School C charged the theater group 10% of the ticket sales and a fixed fee of $200. How much money did School C charge the theater group for use of its facility?

    A. $180
    B. $200
    C. $210
    D. $218
    E. $380

16. What is the difference between the median and the mean number of tickets sold at the 5 schools?

    F. 75
    G. 65
    H. 50
    J. 40
    K. 15

17. What is the area, in square decimeters, of a right triangle with side lengths of 10 dm, 26 dm, and 24 dm ?

    A. 432
    B. 312
    C. 260
    D. 240
    E. 120

2 △ △ △ △ △ △ △ △ △ **2**

18. The mean of a list of 7 numbers is 85. The first 6 numbers on the list are 82, 93, 68, 93, 70, and 98. What is the 7th number on the list?

  F. 83
  G. 84
  H. 90
  J. 91
  K. 93

DO YOUR FIGURING HERE.

19. Which of the following is the sine of the smallest angle in a right triangle with side lengths 7, 24, and 25 inches, respectively?

  A. $\dfrac{7}{25}$

  B. $\dfrac{7}{24}$

  C. $\dfrac{24}{25}$

  D. $\dfrac{24}{7}$

  E. $\dfrac{25}{7}$

20. In the figure shown below, all angles are right angles, and the side lengths given are in feet. What is the area, in square feet, of the figure?

  F. 49
  G. 71
  H. 86
  J. 105
  K. 120

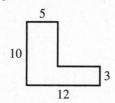

21. A triangle has a perimeter of 26 cm and sides of length x cm, $(x + 3)$ cm, and $(x + 5)$ cm. What is the value of x ?

  A. 6

  B. $8\frac{2}{3}$

  C. 9

  D. 11

  E. 26

22. A truck sprang a leak in its radiator, which held 480 ounces of fluid when it started to leak. Assuming the truck continues at 35 mph and its radiator leaks 4 ounces of fluid per minute, how many *miles* will the truck travel before the radiator is empty?

  F. 13.7
  G. 17.5
  H. 35.0
  J. 70.0
  K. 120.0

GO ON TO THE NEXT PAGE.

2 △ △ △ △ △ △ △ △ △ **2**

23. An ice cream shop sells ice cream cones with exactly 1 of 3 ice cream flavors in the cone. The 3 flavors are vanilla, chocolate, and strawberry. Last Saturday, the shop sold 42 cones. It sold 11 more with chocolate than with vanilla and 2 more with vanilla than with strawberry. How many cones with strawberry ice cream did the shop sell that Saturday?

A. 9
B. 11
C. 14
D. 20
E. 27

24. In △ABC below, D is the midpoint of $\overline{CB}$, ∠ABC is a right angle, AB = 8 m, and AC = 10 m. What is AD, in meters?

F. $\sqrt{41}$
G. $\sqrt{73}$
H. $\sqrt{82}$
J. $\sqrt{91}$
K. $\sqrt{105}$

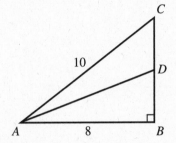

25. Lyman has plotted 5 points in the standard (x,y) coordinate plane below. He then plots a new point as follows: the x-coordinate of the new point is the mean of the x-coordinates of the 5 points already plotted; the y-coordinate of the new point is the mean of the y-coordinates of the 5 points already plotted. Which of the following ordered pairs gives the coordinates of Lyman's new point?

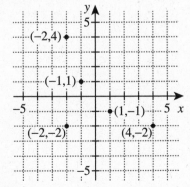

A. (−2,−2)
B. (−1,−1)
C. (0, 0)
D. (1, 1)
E. (2, 2)

GO ON TO THE NEXT PAGE.

2 △ △ △ △ △ △ △ △ △ 2

26. The 1st and 2nd terms of a certain geometric sequence are 10 and −5, respectively. What is the 5th term of the geometric sequence?

F. $-\dfrac{5}{8}$

G. $-\dfrac{5}{16}$

H. $\dfrac{5}{8}$

J. $\dfrac{5}{16}$

K. $\dfrac{5}{32}$

27. Alani works 8 hours per day 5 days each week at a custom embroidery shop. Each day Alani is paid either $1.00 per shirt that she stitches or $10.00 per hour, whichever daily amount is higher. Alani stitched the following numbers of shirts: 60 on Monday, 52 on Tuesday, 85 on Wednesday, 80 on Thursday, and 90 on Friday. What is Alani's total pay for these 5 days?

A. $367.00
B. $400.00
C. $415.00
D. $457.70
E. $587.20

28. Which of the following most precisely describes the roots of the equation $5x^2 + 7x + 2 = 0$?

F. 1 rational (double) root
G. 1 irrational (double) root
H. 2 rational roots
J. 2 irrational roots
K. 2 complex roots (with nonzero imaginary parts)

29. Paula is planning a course for a bike race. The course is in the shape of a right triangle, as shown below. Participants will begin at A, ride directly to B, then directly to C, and directly back to A. Paula wants to put a rest stop at the halfway point on the course. How many miles past B will the rest stop be?

A. 3

B. $6\dfrac{1}{2}$

C. 8

D. 10

E. 13

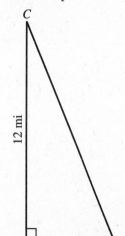

DO YOUR FIGURING HERE.

GO ON TO THE NEXT PAGE.

2 △ △ △ △ △ △ △ △ △ **2**

30. Adams High School has 120 students, and $\frac{1}{3}$ of the students are taking Literature. Of the students NOT taking Literature, $\frac{1}{4}$ are taking Composition. No students are taking both Literature and Composition. How many students are taking Composition?

F. 10
G. 20
H. 30
J. 40
K. 80

DO YOUR FIGURING HERE.

31. For what value of x is the equation $\sqrt{x} + \sqrt{9} = \sqrt{36}$ true?

A. 2
B. 3
C. 4
D. 9
E. 27

32. In the right triangle △ABC shown below, the length of $\overline{BC}$ is 12 feet and $\sin A = \frac{3}{4}$. What is the length, in feet, of $\overline{AC}$?

F. 2
G. 4
H. $4\sqrt{7}$
J. 16
K. 20

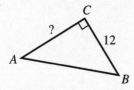

33. What integer does $3(\log_2 16)$ equal?

A. 12
B. 24
C. 64
D. 96
E. 768

34. A bag contains several marbles. On 3 successive draws with replacement, a red marble is drawn from the bag each time. Which of the following statements *must* be true about the marbles in the bag?

F. At least 1 marble is red.
G. Exactly 1 marble is red.
H. Exactly 3 marbles are red.
J. All the marbles are red.
K. The bag contains more red marbles than marbles of other colors.

GO ON TO THE NEXT PAGE.

2 △ △ △ △ △ △ △ △ △ **2**

Use the following information to answer questions 35–37.

Students and adults from Western High School visited an amusement park on a field trip. The amusement park charged $25 for each adult ticket and $20 for each student ticket. Before the trip, the students were given this information about the Happy Dragon roller coaster: the average speed of the roller coaster is 50 miles per hour, and 1 ride on the roller coaster track is completed in 2.25 minutes. A graph showing the height above level ground, in feet, with respect to the time into the ride, in seconds, is given below.

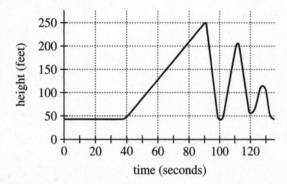

35. Which of the following values is closest to the total distance traveled, in miles, during 1 complete ride on the roller coaster track?

  A. 0.8
  B. 1.9
  C. 2.3
  D. 2.7
  E. 9.4

36. The roller coaster is at a height of at least 235 feet for a total of 5 seconds during each complete ride. Which of the following is closest to the percent of the time during a complete ride that the roller coaster is at a height of at least 235 feet?

  F. 1%
  G. 4%
  H. 19%
  J. 33%
  K. 45%

37. Which of the following values is closest to the average slope, in feet per second, of the graph on the interval between 40 seconds and 90 seconds?

  A. $\dfrac{1}{4}$

  B. $\dfrac{7}{9}$

  C. $2\dfrac{1}{4}$

  D. $2\dfrac{7}{9}$

  E. 4

GO ON TO THE NEXT PAGE.

2 △ △ △ △ △ △ △ △ △ **2**

38. The value of $x^5(0.5x^2 + 2.5x + 6)$ is between which of the following numbers when $x = 10$?

    F. 5×10^4 and 6×10^4

    G. 8×10^4 and 9×10^4

    H. 5×10^6 and 6×10^6

    J. 8×10^6 and 9×10^6

    K. 1×10^7 and 1×10^8

DO YOUR FIGURING HERE.

39. For which of the following data sets is the difference between the mean and the median the greatest?

    A. $\{10, 10, 10, 10\}$

    B. $\{10, 10, 15, 20\}$

    C. $\{10, 15, 15, 15\}$

    D. $\{10, 15, 15, 100\}$

    E. $\{10, 20, 90, 100\}$

40. Pablo has a deck and pool in his backyard. The deck's shape is a rectangle with a semicircle removed and is shown shaded in the figure below. The lengths of the straight sides of the deck are given in feet. Pablo plans to cover the top of the deck with stain. To decide how much stain to purchase, he needs to find the area of the top of the deck. To the nearest square foot, what is the area of the top of the deck?

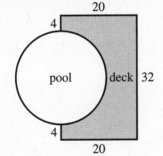

    F. 110
    G. 226
    H. 238
    J. 332
    K. 414

41. A 3-foot-wide brick sidewalk is laid around a rectangular swimming pool. The outside edge of the sidewalk measures 30 feet by 40 feet, as shown in the figure below. What is the perimeter, in feet, of the swimming pool?

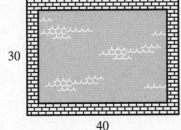

    A.   70
    B.   116
    C.   140
    D.   816
    E. 1,200

GO ON TO THE NEXT PAGE.

42. Given the functions $f(x) = x^2$ and $g(x) = \frac{1}{4-x}$, what is $g(f(x))$?

   F. $\dfrac{1}{4-x^2}$

   G. $\dfrac{1}{(4-x)^2}$

   H. $\dfrac{1}{16-x^2}$

   J. $\dfrac{x^2}{4-x}$

   K. $\dfrac{x^2}{4-x^2}$

DO YOUR FIGURING HERE.

43. A circle has a circumference of $2\pi\sqrt{2}$ feet. What is the area, in square feet, of the circle?

   A. $\pi\sqrt{2}$

   B. $2\pi\sqrt{2}$

   C. 2π

   D. 4π

   E. 8π

44. In the standard (x,y) coordinate plane, the coordinates of the y-intercept of the graph of the function $y = f(x)$ are $(0,-2)$. What are the coordinates of the y-intercept of the graph of the function $y = f(x) - 3$?

   F. $(0,-5)$
   G. $(0,-3)$
   H. $(0,-2)$
   J. $(0, 1)$
   K. $(0, 6)$

45. Which of the following is an equation of a parabola that passes through the 3 points labeled in the standard (x,y) coordinate plane below?

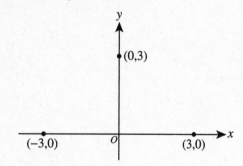

   A. $y = -\frac{1}{3}(x-3)(x+3)$

   B. $y = -(x-3)^2(x+3)$

   C. $y = -(x-3)(x+3)^2$

   D. $y = (x-3)^2(x+3)$

   E. $y = \frac{1}{3}(x-3)(x+3)$

GO ON TO THE NEXT PAGE.

2   **2**

46. As x continually increases in value without bound, the value of $\frac{x}{x+3}$ most closely approaches:

F. 0

G. $\frac{1}{3}$

H. 1

J. 3

K. ∞

DO YOUR FIGURING HERE.

47. Yulan will use a bag of 30 solid-colored marbles for a game in which each player randomly draws marbles from the bag. The number of marbles of each color is shown in the table below.

Color	Number
Blue	10
Red	8
Black	6
White	4
Green	2

Yulan will randomly draw 2 marbles from the bag, one after the other, without replacing the first marble. What is the probability that Yulan will draw a black marble first and a green marble second?

A. $\frac{1}{75}$

B. $\frac{2}{145}$

C. $\frac{4}{15}$

D. $\frac{39}{145}$

E. $\frac{2}{5}$

48. The expression $\frac{2b+c}{b-2c}$ is undefined whenever $b = ?$

F. $-2c$

G. $-\frac{1}{2}c$

H. 0

J. $\frac{1}{2}c$

K. $2c$

GO ON TO THE NEXT PAGE.

2   **2**

49. What number is halfway between $\frac{2}{5}$ and $\frac{8}{7}$?

DO YOUR FIGURING HERE.

- **A.** $\frac{6}{2}$
- **B.** $\frac{5}{6}$
- **C.** $\frac{5}{12}$
- **D.** $\frac{26}{35}$
- **E.** $\frac{27}{35}$

50. A function $f(x)$ is defined as $f(x) = 3^{x^2 - x - 2}$. What 2 real numbers satisfy $f(x) = 1$?
- **F.** −2 and 2
- **G.** −2 and 0
- **H.** −1 and 2
- **J.** −1 and 0
- **K.** 0 and 2

51. The ellipse shown in the standard (x,y) coordinate plane below has equation $\frac{(x-3)^2}{9} + \frac{(y-5)^2}{25} = 1$. Which of the following ordered pairs are the foci of the ellipse?

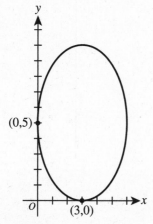

- **A.** (0,5) and (3, 5)
- **B.** (3,0) and (3, 9)
- **C.** (3,0) and (3,10)
- **D.** (3,1) and (3, 9)
- **E.** (3,5) and (6, 5)

GO ON TO THE NEXT PAGE.

2 △ △ △ △ △ △ △ △ △ **2**

52. A basket contains 10 solid-colored balls—2 blue, 3 red, and 5 green. Each ball has a single number printed on it. The blue balls are numbered 1 and 2 (each number is used once), the red balls are numbered 1–3 (each number is used once), and the green balls are numbered 1–5 (each number is used once). A ball will be drawn at random from the basket. What is the probability that the ball that is drawn will be red *or* have a 3 printed on it?

F. $\frac{1}{10}$

G. $\frac{2}{10}$

H. $\frac{3}{10}$

J. $\frac{4}{10}$

K. $\frac{5}{10}$

DO YOUR FIGURING HERE.

53. In the figure below, the given side lengths of $\triangle ABC$ are in inches. What is the area, in square inches, of $\triangle ABC$?

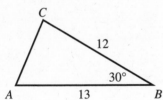

A. 30

B. 39

C. $39\sqrt{3}$

D. 60

E. 78

54. There are 66 calories in 15 grams of grated Parmesan cheese, and 59% of those calories are from fat. When measuring Parmesan cheese, 5 grams is equal to 1 tablespoon. Which of the following is closest to the number of calories from fat per tablespoon of grated Parmesan cheese?

F. 3
G. 8
H. 9
J. 13
K. 22

GO ON TO THE NEXT PAGE.

DO YOUR FIGURING HERE.

55. In the diagram below, B, F, and H are on $\overline{AC}$, $\overline{AE}$, and $\overline{BF}$, respectively, and $\overline{GH} \perp \overline{BF}$. The area of square $ABGF$ is $\frac{1}{4}$ the area of square $ACDE$. What percent of the area of $ACDE$ does the shaded portion represent?

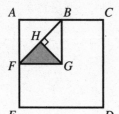

   A.   0.0625%
   B.   0.125%
   C.   0.25%
   D.   6.25%
   E.   12.5%

56. In a data set of 10 distinct values, the single largest value is replaced with a much greater value to form a new data set. Which of the following statements is true about the values of the mean and median for the new data set as compared to the mean and median of the original data set?

   F.   The mean will increase; the median will stay the same.
   G.   The mean will stay the same; the median will increase.
   H.   The mean and median will both stay the same.
   J.   The mean and median will both increase.
   K.   Using the given information, the means and medians of the 2 data sets cannot be compared.

57. Valley High School and Mountain High School have decided that selected students will attend a daytime theatrical performance that costs $5 for each teacher and $3 for each student. One teacher and 10 students from Valley High will attend, and 2 teachers and 25 students from Mountain High will attend. Which of the following matrix products represents the ticket costs, in dollars, for each high school?

   A. $\begin{bmatrix} 5 & 3 \end{bmatrix} \begin{bmatrix} 1 & 2 \\ 10 & 25 \end{bmatrix}$

   B. $\begin{bmatrix} 5 & 3 \end{bmatrix} \begin{bmatrix} 1 & 10 \\ 25 & 2 \end{bmatrix}$

   C. $\begin{bmatrix} 5 & 3 \end{bmatrix} \begin{bmatrix} 1 & 25 \\ 2 & 10 \end{bmatrix}$

   D. $\begin{bmatrix} 5 \\ 3 \end{bmatrix} \begin{bmatrix} 1 & 2 \\ 10 & 25 \end{bmatrix}$

   E. $\begin{bmatrix} 5 \\ 3 \end{bmatrix} \begin{bmatrix} 1 & 10 \\ 2 & 25 \end{bmatrix}$

GO ON TO THE NEXT PAGE.

2 △ △ △ △ △ △ △ △ △ **2**

58. Karie is inventing a new notation in math. She has decided to use $n\downarrow$ to denote the sum of the first n positive integers. For example, $5\downarrow$ means $5 + 4 + 3 + 2 + 1$. Karie has written 3 statements that she is investigating as possible properties of $n\downarrow$.

I. $n\downarrow + (n + 1) = (n + 1)\downarrow$
II. $n\downarrow + n\downarrow = (2n)\downarrow$
III. $(n^2)\downarrow = (n\downarrow)^2$

Which of these statements, if any, is(are) true for all positive integers n ?

F. I only
G. II only
H. III only
J. I, II, and III
K. None

DO YOUR FIGURING HERE.

59. Rey wants to make an open box as shown below, using a square piece of cardboard. He intends to cut a 2-inch square from each corner of the cardboard and fold the cardboard along the lines shown to form the sides. The resulting box will have a volume of 72 cubic inches. What are the dimensions, in inches, of the original piece of cardboard?

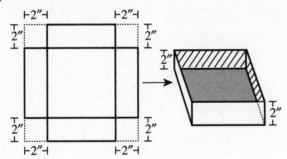

A. 6×6
B. 7×7
C. 8×8
D. 9×9
E. 10×10

60. Which of the following quadratic equations has the complex number $\left(1 + \sqrt{-1}\right)$ as a solution?

F. $x^2 + 1 = 0$
G. $x^2 + x + 1 = 0$
H. $x^2 - x + 1 = 0$
J. $x^2 + 2x - 2 = 0$
K. $x^2 - 2x + 2 = 0$

END OF TEST 2

STOP! DO NOT TURN THE PAGE UNTIL TOLD TO DO SO.

DO NOT RETURN TO THE PREVIOUS TEST.

3   3

READING TEST
35 Minutes — 40 Questions

DIRECTIONS: There are several passages in this test. Each passage is accompanied by several questions. After reading a passage, choose the best answer to each question and fill in the corresponding oval on your answer document. You may refer to the passages as often as necessary.

Passage I

LITERARY NARRATIVE: This passage is adapted from the book *Flower Confidential* by Amy Stewart (©2007 by Amy Stewart).

"Holland" and "the Netherlands" refer to the same country.

I woke up at 5 a.m. and stared at the ceiling of my Amsterdam hotel room. Outside, the canal boats, which were rented to rowdy college students, had just gone quiet. This was a city of late risers. I got dressed and
5 walked gingerly through the lobby, not wanting to wake the innkeeper who slept on the ground floor, and stepped into the dark, empty streets. The fact is that if you want to go see someone in the flower trade, this is the hour at which you must rise. Even then, when you
10 finally show up at 6 or 7 a.m., blinking in the sudden daylight and trying to remember why you scheduled the meeting in the first place, the person you've gone to meet will look impatient, as though half the day is wasted already.

15   I was on my way to Aalsmeer to see the famous Dutch flower auction. It's known around the world as a remarkably high-tech, high-speed way to sell flowers, but it had modest beginnings: In a café outside of Amsterdam in 1911 some growers came up with the idea of
20 holding an auction to give them more control over how their flowers were priced and sold. They called their auction Bloemenlust. It was not long before a competing auction sprang up nearby—the history of flower markets everywhere is that as soon as there is one, there
25 are two—and each day as the auctions ended, flowers were piled onto bicycles and boats to be delivered along Holland's narrow canals and even narrower streets. This arrangement continued until 1968, the two auctions thriving nearly side by side, until they finally merged
30 and became what is known today as Bloemenveiling Aalsmeer, the largest of a handful of major flower auctions going on year-round in the Netherlands.

The bus to Aalsmeer took me through the shuttered streets of Amsterdam and headed south, past the
35 airport. The world seemed to be coming to life at last, and on the road we passed dozens of trucks—some of them plastered with the same grower and wholesaler logos you'd see in Miami—carrying flowers to and from the auction. This next phase of a flower's life,
40 after it leaves the grower and before it settles into a vase on someone's hall table, is remarkable for both its duration and its complexity. A flower can spend a week making its way through a maze of warehouses, airports, auctions, and wholesale markets, and it will emerge
45 from this exhausting journey looking almost as fresh as the day it was picked.

The existence of this auction highlights one major difference between flowers destined for the European market and those sold in the United States. The flowers
50 that I saw arriving in Miami were headed in every direction at once: they were going by truck, rail, and plane to wholesale markets, distribution centers, bouquet makers, retailers, and even directly to customers. There is not a single, centralized market for flowers in
55 the United States. But the flowers that come into Schiphol Airport outside of Amsterdam, the major port of entry for European flowers, are almost all going to Aalsmeer. This is the very center of the flower trade, handling most of the flowers sold on the European
60 market and some of the goods going to Russia, China, Japan, and even the United States. The flowers going up for auction come from Kenya, Zimbabwe, Israel, Colombia, Ecuador, and European countries, making this a sort of global stopping-off point for most of the
65 industry. Every flower market around the world watches the Dutch auction, which acts as a sort of engine for the trade, setting prices and standards worldwide. If you want to follow a flower to market, you'll end up here eventually.

70   By the time the bus pulled into the large circular driveway at the public entrance to the auction, the day really was half over. Flowers and plants had been arriving since midnight, and bidding started before dawn. I stepped off the bus into a kind of floral rush hour:
75 trucks roaring past, people racing from one end of the complex to another, the morning sun glaring down. This place is a behemoth in the small town of Aalsmeer. It employs ten thousand people in a town of just twenty thousand and occupies almost 450 acres, an area larger
80 than Walt Disney World's Magic Kingdom and Epcot theme parks combined. In fact, the auction is like a city in itself, one that runs twenty-four hours a day. All the major growers and wholesalers keep an office, and maybe a warehouse and a loading dock, at Aalsmeer. A
85 full 20 percent of the cut flowers in the world are sold at this very spot, and about half of the world's cut-flower supply moves through the Dutch auction system.

GO ON TO THE NEXT PAGE.

3 ▬▬▬▬▬▬▬▬▬▬▬▬▬▬▬▬▬▬▬▬ **3**

1. Which of the following events referred to in the passage happened first chronologically?

   A. The author woke up at 5:00 a.m.
   B. The students on the canal boats quieted down.
   C. The author's bus passed the Amsterdam airport.
   D. Flowers and plants started arriving at the auction.

2. The main idea of the first paragraph is that:

   F. the author is not accustomed to getting up very early in the morning.
   G. the author is surprised by how quiet Amsterdam is early in the morning.
   H. though Amsterdam in general is made up of late risers, the local flower trade is busiest in early morning.
   J. because Amsterdam is usually bustling with activity, it is advisable to meet with people in the local flower trade early in the morning.

3. The author most strongly suggests that when meeting with a person in the flower trade in the morning, that person will look impatient because:

   A. people in the flower trade are generally late risers.
   B. he or she is anxious about wasting time.
   C. he or she can't remember why the meeting was scheduled in the first place.
   D. people living in Amsterdam are always on the go.

4. The information between the dashes in lines 23–25 most strongly suggests that flower markets generally tend to:

   F. function best in small cities.
   G. merge if both markets are successful.
   H. operate in a competitive atmosphere.
   J. suffer when competing vendors appear.

5. Based on the author's discussion of the "exhausting journey" (line 45) experienced by flowers sent to auction, the author would most likely agree with the idea that these flowers:

   A. are surprisingly resilient.
   B. are picked past their prime.
   C. have remarkably complex biological needs.
   D. should be shipped by plane to remain fresh.

6. Based on the passage, the main way the US flower market differs from the European flower market is that:

   F. flowers in the United States are usually shipped directly to customers.
   G. flowers in the United States are transported by truck, rail, and plane.
   H. there are no wholesale flower markets in the United States.
   J. there is no centralized flower market in the United States.

7. As it is used in line 18, the word *modest* most nearly means:

   A. bashful.
   B. simple.
   C. middling.
   D. decent.

8. Details in the third paragraph (lines 33–46) indicate that one similarity between the flower industry in the United States and the flower industry in Holland is that both:

   F. have well-known high-tech flower auctions.
   G. are supplied primarily by growers in Europe.
   H. conduct major flower auctions all year long.
   J. use some of the same growers and wholesalers.

9. The author refers to the Magic Kingdom and Epcot theme parks mainly to:

   A. indicate that the Aalsmeer market is more crowded than the two theme parks combined.
   B. provide support for the idea that the Aalsmeer market is a lot of fun to attend.
   C. suggest that the Aalsmeer market employs as many people as the two theme parks do.
   D. help emphasize the sprawling space the Aalsmeer market occupies.

10. According to the passage, which of the following numbers of flowers is sold at the Aalsmeer auction?

   F. Ten thousand flowers per day
   G. Half of the flowers grown in Holland
   H. Twenty percent of the world's cut flowers
   J. Eighty percent of the flowers in the European market

GO ON TO THE NEXT PAGE.

3 ▬▬▬▬▬▬▬▬▬▬▬▬▬▬▬▬▬▬▬▬ **3**

Passage II

SOCIAL SCIENCE: This passage is adapted from the article "The Reluctant President" by Ron Chernow (©2011 by Ron Chernow).

On February 4, 1789, the 69 members of the Electoral College made George Washington the only president to be unanimously elected, but Congress was unable to meet until April to make the choice official.

The Congressional delay in certifying George Washington's election as president only allowed more time for his doubts to fester as he considered the herculean task ahead. He savored his wait as a welcome
5 "reprieve," he told his former comrade in arms and future Secretary of War Henry Knox, adding that his "movements to the chair of government will be accompanied with feelings not unlike those of a culprit who is going to the place of his execution." His "peaceful
10 abode" at Mount Vernon, his fears that he lacked the requisite skills for the presidency, the "ocean of difficulties" facing the country—all gave him pause on the eve of his momentous trip to New York. In a letter to his friend Edward Rutledge, he claimed that, in accept-
15 ing the presidency, he had given up "all expectations of private happiness in this world."

The day after Congress counted the electoral votes, declaring Washington the first president, it dispatched Charles Thomson, the secretary of Congress, to
20 bear the official announcement to Mount Vernon. The legislators had chosen a fine emissary. A well-rounded man, known for his work in astronomy and mathematics, the Irish-born Thomson couldn't have relished the trying journey to Virginia, which was "much impeded
25 by tempestuous weather, bad roads, and the many large rivers I had to cross." Yet he rejoiced that the new president would be Washington, whom he venerated as someone singled out by Providence to be "the savior and father" of the country. Having known Thomson
30 since the Continental Congress, Washington esteemed him as a faithful public servant and exemplary patriot.

Around noon on April 14, 1789, Washington flung open the door at Mount Vernon and greeted his visitor with a cordial embrace. Once in the privacy of the man-
35 sion, he and Thomson conducted a stiff verbal minuet, each man reading from a prepared statement. Thomson began by declaring, "I am honored with the commands of the Senate to wait upon your Excellency with the information of your being elected to the office of Presi-
40 dent of the United States of America" by a unanimous vote. He read aloud a letter from Senator John Langdon of New Hampshire, the president pro tempore. "Suffer me, sir, to indulge the hope that so auspicious a mark of public confidence will meet your approbation and be
45 considered as a sure pledge of the affection and support you are to expect from a free and enlightened people." There was something deferential, even slightly servile, in Langdon's tone, as if he feared that Washington might renege on his promise and refuse to take the job.
50 Thus was greatness once again thrust upon George Washington.

Any student of Washington's life might have predicted that he would acknowledge his election in a short, self-effacing speech full of disclaimers. "While I
55 realize the arduous nature of the task which is conferred on me and feel my inability to perform it," he replied to Thomson, "I wish there may not be reason for regretting the choice. All I can promise is only that which can be accomplished by an honest zeal." This sentiment of
60 modesty jibed so perfectly with Washington's private letters that it could not have been feigned: he wondered whether he was fit for the post, so unlike anything he had ever done. The hopes for republican government, he knew, rested in his hands. As commander in chief of
65 the Continental Army, he had been able to wrap himself in a self-protective silence, but the presidency would leave him with no place to hide and expose him to public censure as nothing before.

Because the vote counting had been long delayed,
70 Washington, 57, felt the crush of upcoming public business and decided to set out promptly for New York on April 16, accompanied in his elegant carriage by Thomson and aide David Humphreys. His diary entry conveys a sense of foreboding: "About ten o'clock, I
75 bade adieu to Mount Vernon, to private life, and to domestic felicity and, with a mind oppressed with more anxious and painful sensations than I have words to express, set out for New York . . . with the best dispositions to render service to my country in obedience to its
80 call, but with less hope of answering its expectations." Waving goodbye was Martha Washington, who wouldn't join him until mid-May. She watched her husband of 30 years depart with a mixture of bittersweet sensations, wondering "when or whether he will ever
85 come home again." She had long doubted the wisdom of this final act in his public life. "I think it was much too late for him to go into public life again," she told her nephew, "but it was not to be avoided."

11. Which of the following statements best captures the broad, general message of the passage?

   A. The most effective leader pairs strong inner confidence with public displays of humility.

   B. Leaving a comfortable, familiar life for the unknown will likely have great rewards.

   C. Even a leader who is strongly supported by the public may have deep, private insecurities.

   D. Electing someone who is not prepared to lead may have dangerous consequences.

GO ON TO THE NEXT PAGE.

3 ████████████████████████████████████ **3**

12. One function in the passage of including information about Mount Vernon and Martha Washington is to create a contrast between George Washington's:

F. carefree, casual demeanor around his family and his stern aspect with advisors and aides.

G. idyllic, established home life and the uncertainty of what was to come in his public life.

H. restlessness at home and his calm, collected sense of industriousness as president.

J. enjoyment of a private home life and his dislike of working without close advisors in government.

13. As it is used in line 35, the phrase "stiff verbal minuet" refers to the interaction between George Washington and Thomson as Washington:

A. writes a letter to Langdon, the president pro tempore.

B. excuses himself from Thomson so that he may say goodbye to his wife, Martha.

C. is officially told that he has been elected president of the United States and accepts the position.

D. formally resigns from his position as commander in chief of the army and appoints a replacement.

14. The passage author argues that the letter read to George Washington on April 14, 1789, suggests Langdon's concern that:

F. Washington would be forced by Congress to confer his duties to a president pro tempore for several months.

G. Washington had been behaving inappropriately as commander in chief of the army.

H. the problems facing the country were insurmountable for any new president.

J. there was a chance that Washington would reject the opportunity to become president.

15. The passage characterizes which of the following people as expressing a subtle acknowledgement of George Washington's burden?

A. Knox

B. Langdon

C. Rutledge

D. Thomson

16. According to the passage, the congressional delay in certifying George Washington's election allowed Washington time to:

F. steep himself in his doubts and fears, causing them to grow.

G. share with others his hopes for and confidence in the republican government.

H. closely consider the herculean task ahead, which eased some of his worry.

J. confer with his aides about the difficulties facing the country.

17. The passage indicates that Thomson's journey to Mount Vernon was made difficult by:

A. the lack of a party to accompany him, which left him vulnerable to bandits.

B. his need to return as quickly as possible to his duties as the secretary of Congress.

C. terrible weather and a route that included river crossings and bad roads.

D. his miscalculation of the route, which led to a long, arduous detour.

18. As it is used in line 43, the word *mark* most nearly means:

F. boundary.

G. sign.

H. impact.

J. stain.

19. The passage most strongly implies that while Washington was commander in chief of the army, one way he had preserved his good reputation was by:

A. giving speeches.

B. publishing pamphlets.

C. writing letters.

D. remaining silent.

20. The passage author makes clear Martha Washington's view that her husband's return to public life was:

F. an inevitable event for him.

G. a subtle rejection of his private life with her.

H. an inexcusable decision for him.

J. a source of pride for her.

GO ON TO THE NEXT PAGE.

3   **3**

Passage III

HUMANITIES: Passage A is adapted from the article "A Million Little Pieces" by Andrea K. Scott (©2012 by Condé Nast Publications). Passage B is adapted from the article "Everything in Its Right Place" by Karen Rosenberg (©2011 by The New York Times).

Passage A by Andrea K. Scott

The artist Sarah Sze stood in the foyer on the second floor of the Asia Society, on the Upper East Side, amid dozens of crates, plastic storage bins, plastic tubs, and plastic bags. It was a late afternoon in Decem-
5 ber, and she and six assistants were completing the installation of eight new sculptures. The process was so labor-intensive that it had taken more than three weeks.

Sze arranges everyday objects into sculptural installations of astonishing intricacy. She joins things
10 manufactured to help build other things (ladders, levels, winches, extension cords) with hundreds of common-place items (cotton swabs, push-pins, birthday candles, aspirin tablets), creating elaborate compositions that extend from gallery walls, creep into corners, and
15 surge toward ceilings. Duchamp paved the way for Sze's work when he made a sculpture by mounting a bicycle wheel on a wooden stool. But her virtuosic creations are equally indebted to the explosive energy of Bernini's Baroque masterpiece "The Ecstasy of
20 St. Teresa," a marble statue that seems to ripple with movement.

Sze's show was about the relationships between landscape and architecture, and sculpture and line. She walked from the foyer into the galleries, and stood by a
25 floor-to-ceiling window that had been concealed by a wall for a decade—the museum had uncovered it at her request. She began to confer with her studio manager, Mike Barnett. Sze was wondering about a branch that she had placed in the installation by the window, after
30 pruning it from her roof-top garden, in downtown Man-hattan. It rose from the floor like a sapling emerging from a crack in the sidewalk. Twilight had turned the window into a mirror, but in daylight the branch would compete with a view of Park Avenue median greenery,
35 traffic, and apartment buildings.

"There's a nighttime view and a daytime view," she said to Barnett. "I want that to be a plus, not a minus. Is this getting lost?"

Barnett said, "I think it works."

40 There was a pause so long that it should have been awkward. Sze finally said, "Even if it's a loose end, that could be interesting. I like that it looks like a frag-ment—like it could just drift away."

Passage B by Karen Rosenberg

"Infinite Line," Sarah Sze's midcareer solo show at
45 Asia Society Museum, promised a new angle on Ms. Sze's mesmerizing, minutely detailed installations. And it delivers one, though the art—much of it made for the occasion—doesn't always rise to the challenge.

The show makes the case that Ms. Sze, who is
50 Chinese-American, has been profoundly influenced by many forms of Asian art. It also emphasizes her draw-ings, which have rarely been exhibited, and encourages you to see her three-dimensional artworks as drawings in space.

55 Implicitly, it de-emphasizes the prosaic nature of her art materials: the cotton swabs, toothpicks, bottle caps and other throwaway objects that she fashions, with gee-whiz structural ingenuity, into rambling land-scapes and galactic spirals. Over the years viewers
60 (myself included) have had a tendency to focus on all of this stuff—to see Ms. Sze's art as embodying a quintes-sentially American consumerism.

"Infinite Line" presents a more nuanced, intellec-tual and worldly artist: one who talks about space like
65 an architect and vision like an ophthalmologist, who rhapsodizes about the shifting perspective in Chinese painting and makes her own Asian-inspired drawings on long scrolls of paper.

But while Ms. Sze says some fascinating things in
70 a catalog interview, she's not at her best in these gal-leries. Nothing here is quite up to the level of her solo at the Tanya Bonakdar Gallery last year, which used cantilevered shelves laden with rocks, plants and office supplies to evoke a topsy-turvy green house or curiosity
75 cabinet.

That's especially true of the works on paper, which are installed in a separate room and look physically and spiritually cut off from Ms. Sze's signature installa-tions. Most of them find her in doodle mode, drawing
80 clusters of architecture and tiny figures that can be expanded or contracted to suit any scale or purpose.

Pure drawing, as a medium, does not seem to excite Ms. Sze. It takes a hint of found objects, or a flir-tation with the third dimension, to bring out her imagi-
85 nation, as in the collage "Guggenheim as a Ruin," which envisions a crumbling, entropic version of that museum, or the pop-up drawing "Notepad," whose laser-cut and folded pages form a series of cascading fire escapes.

3 3

Questions 21–25 ask about Passage A.

21. In Passage A, the first paragraph (lines 1–7) functions mainly to emphasize the:

A. leadership skills Sze demonstrated in relegating work to her assistants at the Asia Society.

B. ingenuity and problem solving Sze used to create her eight sculptures at the Asia Society.

C. amount of time and materials Sze needed to create her eight sculptures at the Asia Society.

D. amount of space Sze's eight sculptures took up on the second floor of the Asia Society.

22. Which of the following sculptural installations would be most conceptually similar to Sze's sculptural installations discussed in the second paragraph of Passage A (lines 8–21)?

F. An oversized tricycle hanging above a sofa

G. A large slab of marble with streams of water rippling over it

H. Rubber bands and nails joined together to form a network of cables

J. Paper clips strewn about randomly on a gallery floor

23. As it is used in line 13, the word *elaborate* most nearly means:

A. luxurious.

B. exact.

C. overdone.

D. complicated.

24. It can most reasonably be inferred from Passage A that the main reason Sze requested that the floor-to-ceiling window be uncovered is that she wanted the window to contribute to her exploration of the:

F. relationship between landscape and architecture.

G. influences of consumerism on cultural constructs.

H. differences between Asian and Western art.

J. effects of urban sprawl on the environment.

25. In Passage A, the author most likely references Bernini's "The Ecstasy of St. Teresa" in order to emphasize that Sze's installations appear:

A. antiquated.

B. symmetrical.

C. ornate.

D. lively.

Questions 26 and 27 ask about Passage B.

26. The author of Passage B is most critical of which artworks in Sze's show "Infinite Line"?

F. Two-dimensional works on paper

G. Three-dimensional works on paper

H. Sculptural installations

J. Collages

27. As it is used in line 57, the word *fashions* most nearly means:

A. accommodates.

B. initiates.

C. combines.

D. wears.

Questions 28–30 ask about both passages.

28. Which of the following statements best captures a difference in the purposes of the passages?

F. Passage A provides a critique of how Sze conceptualizes her art shows, while Passage B provides a comparison between Sze and other Asian American artists.

G. Passage A provides a glimpse into Sze's creative process, while Passage B provides a critique of her art show "Infinite Line."

H. Passage A provides a comparison of Sze's personal and public personas, while Passage B provides a narrative concerning how Sze discovered Asian art.

J. Passage A provides an overview of Sze's development as an artist, while Passage B provides an interpretation of Sze's artwork.

29. Compared to Passage B, Passage A provides more information regarding how Sze:

A. places objects within a gallery space.

B. feels about the artists Duchamp and Bernini.

C. reacts to critical interpretations of her artwork.

D. incorporates classical Chinese imagery into her sculptural installations.

30. The authors of Passage A and Passage B both praise Sze for her use of:

F. organic material in her collages.

G. detail in her sculptural installations.

H. proportion in her works on paper.

J. natural light in her sculpture gardens.

GO ON TO THE NEXT PAGE.

3 ━━━━━━━━━━━━━━━━━━━━━━━━━━━━ **3**

Passage IV

NATURAL SCIENCE: This passage is adapted from the article "The Strangest Bird" by R. Ewan Fordyce and Daniel T. Ksepka (©2012 by Scientific American).

That the earliest penguins have turned up in New Zealand is probably no coincidence. Until humans arrived, less than 1,000 years ago, the islands there formed a temperate seabird paradise on the margins of
5   the South Pacific and Southern oceans. The region was free of terrestrial predatory mammals and afforded space for breeding colonies, with abundant food in the surrounding seas.

Geologic evidence suggests that the area would
10 have been equally conducive to the seabird way of life at the end of the Cretaceous. New Zealand today is the largest exposed area of a submerged mini continent known as Zealandia that broke off from the ancient supercontinent of Gondwana perhaps 85 million years
15 ago. Thus liberated, Zealandia drifted northeast into the Pacific, carrying plants and animals, including dinosaurs, to its resting spot about halfway between the South Pole and tropics. As Zealandia drifted, it cooled and sank. Shallow seas flooded the land, and a broad
20 continental shelf formed around its perimeter. Despite its isolation from other landmasses, Zealandia did not emerge from the end-Cretaceous extinction unscathed. Many of its marine and terrestrial organisms perished in that die-off. Yet what was bad for those creatures was
25 good for penguins. With marine reptiles such as mosasaurs and plesiosaurs out of the picture, early penguins could swim the waters around Zealandia free of competition or predation.

Having gotten their sea legs in Zealandia, pen-
30 guins soon expanded their domain dramatically, dispersing across thousands of miles and into new climate zones. Fossils of *Perudyptes devriesi* from Peru show that penguins arrived close to the equator about 42 million years ago, settling in one of the hottest places on
35 earth during one of the hottest times in the planet's history. By 37 million years ago the birds had spread to almost every major landmass in the Southern Hemisphere.

Yet why, after restricting themselves to Zealandia
40 for millions of years, did penguins suddenly start spreading across the Southern Hemisphere around 50 million years ago? Recently Daniel T. Ksepka discovered an important clue to this mystery: a long-overlooked feature on the surface of fossil flipper
45 bones. The humerus bears a series of grooves that are easy to miss among the markings associated with tendons and muscles.

Those grooves form at the spot where a cluster of arteries and veins presses against the humerus. These
50 blood vessels make up a countercurrent heat exchanger called the humeral arterial plexus, which allows penguins to limit heat loss through the flippers and to maintain their core body temperature in cold water. In live penguins, hot blood leaving the heart gets cooled
55 by the plexus before reaching the flipper tip, and cold blood returning from the flipper gets warmed before approaching the heart.

The identity of the grooves on the fossil flipper bones shed some surprising light on the origin of pen-
60 guin thermoregulation. One of the most amazing aspects of modern penguin biology is the birds' ability to tolerate extreme cold. One would logically assume that the plexus evolved as an adaptation to frigid environments. But fossils suggest otherwise. Penguins such
65 as the *Delphinornis* from Antarctica show that this feature evolved at least 49 million years ago. The early *Waimanu* penguins from Zealandia show no hint of the trait at 58 million years ago, however. The plexus therefore must have evolved in the intervening time, when
70 the earth was far warmer than it is today. Back then, Antarctica lacked permanent ice sheets and instead offered a temperate forested environment; Zealandia was even toastier.

What use did early penguins have for a heat-
75 conserving plexus in this greenhouse world? Although sea-surface temperatures were high, early penguins probably foraged in cool upwelling regions, which are rich in nutrients and thus support a bounty of prey, including fish and squid. But because heat is lost more
80 quickly in water than air, a warm-blooded animal such as the penguin risks going into hypothermia even in warm seas if the water is below core body temperature. Reducing heat loss through the flipper would have helped them conserve body heat on long foraging
85 swims in chilly waters.

The humeral plexus may have also allowed penguins to survive the long open-water journeys by which they initially dispersed from Zealandia to other continents. Only much later would modern penguins co-opt
90 this mechanism to invade the sea ice shelves that formed when the planet cooled.

31. One main purpose of the passage is to:
   A. analyze why New Zealand has long been an ideal environment for penguins.
   B. compare two leading theories about penguin habitats based on evidence from the fossil record.
   C. present evidence that penguin populations have steadily declined since the late Cretaceous.
   D. describe a particular fossil discovery that led to a better understanding of how penguins evolved.

GO ON TO THE NEXT PAGE.

3 ━━━━━━━━━━━━━━━━━━━━━ **3**

32. Which of the following statements best summarizes the authors' claim about the relationship between the humeral arterial plexus and cold environments?

   F. The early emergence of the humeral arterial plexus allowed penguins to later inhabit cold environments.
   G. The humeral arterial plexus appears to have little to do with penguins' ability to survive in cold environments.
   H. The humeral arterial plexus allows penguins to survive in cold environments by increasing penguins' heart rates.
   J. Once penguins adapted to the sea ice shelves that formed when the planet cooled, they no longer had a need for the humeral arterial plexus.

33. It can reasonably be inferred from the passage that the phrase "what was bad for those creatures" (line 24) refers to:

   A. a change in food sources for early penguins.
   B. the end-Cretaceous die-off of the dinosaurs and other animals.
   C. how Zealandia's isolation from the South Pole affected Zealandia's terrestrial mammals.
   D. seabirds' exposure to new climate zones.

34. According to the passage, about 55 million years ago, how did the average temperatures of Zealandia compare to those of Antarctica?

   F. Zealandia was generally cooler than Antarctica.
   G. Zealandia was generally warmer than Antarctica.
   H. Temperatures in Zealandia were about the same as those in Antarctica.
   J. Temperatures in Zealandia were higher than Antarctica in the summer and lower in the winter.

35. In the passage, the authors conclude that the humeral arterial plexus mechanism emerged in penguins in conjunction with a need to:

   A. survive in new climates closer to the equator.
   B. adapt to a temperate forested environment.
   C. forage in cool upwelling regions of the sea.
   D. swim long distances on warm ocean surfaces.

36. According to the passage, which of the following occurred as Zealandia drifted into the Pacific?

   F. A broad continental shelf formed around Gondwana, making Zealandia more isolated.
   G. Gondwana warmed, becoming a seabird paradise.
   H. Zealandia slowly became completely submerged.
   J. Zealandia's climate cooled and the landmass sank lower in the seas.

37. The passage indicates that penguins living in the Cretaceous faced predation and competition for food from:

   A. marine reptiles.
   B. large fish.
   C. other seabird species.
   D. squid.

38. Based on the passage, which penguin fossil bones yielded the most significant information for the authors' study of penguins?

   F. Feet
   G. Chest
   H. Flippers
   J. Skull

39. As it is used in line 45, the word *bears* most nearly means:

   A. produces.
   B. endures.
   C. exhibits.
   D. merits.

40. The passage most strongly suggests that the markings from the humeral plexus had likely gone unnoticed on fossils because:

   F. modern penguin bones do not have such markings.
   G. the markings are difficult to distinguish from others on the humerus.
   H. the markings easily deteriorate over time.
   J. little scientific research has been devoted to early penguin fossils.

END OF TEST 3

STOP! DO NOT TURN THE PAGE UNTIL TOLD TO DO SO.

DO NOT RETURN TO A PREVIOUS TEST.

4   4

SCIENCE TEST
35 Minutes—40 Questions

DIRECTIONS: There are several passages in this test. Each passage is followed by several questions. After reading a passage, choose the best answer to each question and fill in the corresponding oval on your answer document. You may refer to the passages as often as necessary.

You are NOT permitted to use a calculator on this test.

Passage I

Wood mice (a species of mammal) typically forage for food at night. Their foraging behavior can be affected by environmental factors, including the presence of moonlight and the presence of shelter (such as shrubs). Four students each proposed a hypothesis describing how the foraging behavior of wood mice is affected by the presence of moonlight and shelter. Then they conducted an experiment to test their hypotheses.

Student 1

Wood mice are more likely to forage when moonlight is absent than when moonlight is present. The absence of moonlight decreases the chance that a wood mouse will be captured by a predator. Therefore, the number of wood mouse visits to a foraging site will be greater during the new moon than during the full moon. Shelter has no effect on foraging behavior.

Student 2

Wood mice are more likely to forage at sites with shelter than at sites without shelter. The presence of shelter decreases the chance that a wood mouse will be captured by a predator. Therefore, the number of wood mouse visits to a foraging site will be greater when shelter is present than when shelter is absent. Moonlight has no effect on foraging behavior.

Student 3

Wood mice are more likely to forage at sites with shelter than at sites without shelter, and they are more likely to forage when moonlight is absent than when moonlight is present. Both the presence of shelter and the absence of moonlight decrease the chance that a wood mouse will be captured by a predator. Therefore, the greatest number of wood mouse visits will be to foraging sites with shelter during the new moon.

Student 4

The foraging behavior of wood mice is not affected by the presence of shelter or moonlight. These factors do not affect the chance that a wood mouse will be captured by a predator, and therefore do not affect the number of wood mouse visits to a foraging site.

Experiment

Over the course of several months, the students counted the number of wood mouse visits to a foraging site with shelter and a foraging site without shelter during the new moon and during the full moon (see table).

Shelter present?	Number of visits during new moon	Number of visits during full moon
Yes	1,003	882
No	285	191

Table adapted from Ramón Perea et al., "Moonlight and Shelter Cause Differential Seed Selection and Removal by Rodents." ©2011 by The Association for the Study of Animal Behaviour.

GO ON TO THE NEXT PAGE.

4 ◯ ◯ ◯ ◯ ◯ ◯ ◯ ◯ 4

1. A scientist claimed that adding shrubs to a foraging site will increase the number of wood mouse visits to that site. This claim is consistent with the hypothesis or hypotheses of which of the students?

  A. Student 2 only
  B. Students 1 and 4 only
  C. Students 2 and 3 only
  D. Students 1, 2, 3, and 4

2. Based on Student 3's hypothesis, a wood mouse would be *least* likely to be captured by a predator during the:

  F. new moon at a foraging site with shelter.
  G. new moon at a foraging site without shelter.
  H. full moon at a foraging site with shelter.
  J. full moon at a foraging site without shelter.

3. Consider the results of the experiment, during the new moon and during the full moon, for the site without shelter. Are these results consistent with the hypothesis of Student 1 ?

  A. Yes; there were fewer visits during the new moon than during the full moon.
  B. Yes; there were more visits during the new moon than during the full moon.
  C. No; there were fewer visits during the new moon than during the full moon.
  D. No; there were more visits during the new moon than during the full moon.

4. Before the experiment, which student would most likely have predicted that the number of wood mouse visits would be approximately the same for all the conditions that were tested?

  F. Student 1
  G. Student 2
  H. Student 3
  J. Student 4

5. Over the course of several months, a scientist conducted a study to determine if the number of wood mouse visits to a foraging site varied with moonlight brightness. The results of the study are shown in the following figure.

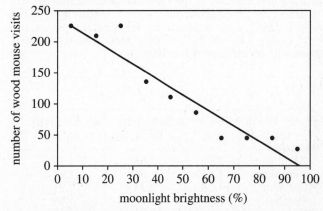

Figure adapted from Ramón Perea et al., "Moonlight and Shelter Cause Differential Seed Selection and Removal by Rodents." ©2011 by The Association for the Study of Animal Behaviour.

These results are consistent with the hypothesis or hypotheses of which of the students?

  A. Student 1 only
  B. Student 4 only
  C. Students 1 and 3 only
  D. Students 2 and 3 only

6. The results of the experiment are most consistent with the hypothesis of which student?

  F. Student 1
  G. Student 2
  H. Student 3
  J. Student 4

7. Which of the following questions was addressed by each of the hypotheses but cannot be directly answered by the results of the experiment?

  A. Does the presence of moonlight and shelter affect the chance that a wood mouse will be captured by a predator?
  B. Does the presence of moonlight and shelter affect the chance that a wood mouse will construct a nest at a foraging site?
  C. Does a foraging site receive more visits from wood mice during a new moon than during a full moon?
  D. Does a foraging site with shelter receive more visits from wood mice than does a foraging site without shelter?

GO ON TO THE NEXT PAGE.

4   **4**

Passage II

Resistivity is the tendency of a material to oppose the flow of an electric current, whereas *conductivity* is the ability of a material to carry an electric current. Table 1 lists, for each of 12 metals at the same temperature, the density (in grams per cubic centimeter, g/cm^3), resistivity (in ohm meters, Ω·m), and conductivity (in siemens per meter, S/m). Figure 1 shows, for 3 of these metals, how resistivity varies with temperature (in kelvins, K).

Table 1			
Metal	Density (g/cm^3)	Resistivity ($\times 10^{-8}$ Ω·m)	Conductivity ($\times 10^7$ S/m)
Aluminum	2.70	2.65	3.77
Beryllium	1.85	3.56	2.81
Calcium	1.54	3.36	2.97
Copper	8.96	1.68	5.96
Gold	19.3	2.21	4.52
Iron	7.87	9.61	1.03
Lithium	0.530	9.28	1.08
Magnesium	1.74	4.39	2.23
Potassium	0.890	7.20	1.39
Silver	10.5	1.59	6.30
Sodium	0.970	4.88	2.05
Tungsten	19.3	5.39	1.86

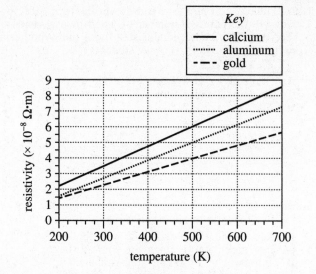

Figure 1

GO ON TO THE NEXT PAGE.

4 ○ ○ ○ ○ ○ ○ ○ ○ **4**

8. According to Figure 1, at a temperature of 600 K, which of calcium, aluminum, and gold has(have) a resistivity greater than 7×10^{-8} Ω·m ?

   F. Calcium only
   G. Aluminum only
   H. Calcium and aluminum only
   J. Calcium and gold only

9. Based on Table 1, of the following 4 metals, which has the greatest ability to carry electric current?

   A. Beryllium
   B. Iron
   C. Magnesium
   D. Tungsten

10. According to Figure 1, approximately how many times as great is the resistivity of aluminum at 600 K than at 320 K ?

   F. $\frac{1}{4}$
   G. $\frac{1}{2}$
   H. 2
   J. 4

11. Suppose that a certain metal has a resistivity of 3.46×10^{-8} Ω·m. Based on Table 1, the conductivity of this metal is most likely closest to which of the following?

   A. 1.69×10^{-7} S/m
   B. 2.89×10^{-7} S/m
   C. 1.69×10^{7} S/m
   D. 2.89×10^{7} S/m

12. When choosing a suitable metal for use in overhead electrical cables, engineers prefer a metal for which the expression (density) × (resistivity) has as small a value as possible. Based on Table 1, which of the following metals would be most suitable for use in an overhead cable?

   F. Aluminum
   G. Copper
   H. Gold
   J. Silver

13. Based on Figure 1, the resistivities of the metals listed in Table 1 were most likely measured at a temperature closest to which of the following?

   A. 200 K
   B. 300 K
   C. 400 K
   D. 500 K

GO ON TO THE NEXT PAGE.

4 ◯ ◯ ◯ ◯ ◯ ◯ ◯ ◯ 4

Passage III

When *Moina micrura* (microscopic aquatic crustaceans) are exposed to unfavorable environmental conditions, they produce *ephippia* (specialized eggs that each contain a dormant embryo). The embryos remain dormant until the ephippia are exposed to favorable environmental conditions that cause the ephippia to hatch. Two experiments examined how pH and light intensity affect the hatching of *M. micrura* ephippia.

Experiment 1

Each of 15 identical beakers received 50 mL of water and 120 freshly laid *M. micrura* ephippia. The beakers were then equally divided into 5 groups (Groups L–P). For each group of beakers, the water was maintained at 1 of 5 different pH values (see Table 1).

Table 1	
Group	pH
L	3.0
M	5.0
N	7.0
O	9.0
P	11.0

Each beaker was then incubated at 27°C and received 12 hr of light per day at a light intensity of 650 lux. At the end of 7 days, the number of ephippia that had hatched in each beaker was counted, and the average number of ephippia hatched in each group was calculated (see Figure 1).

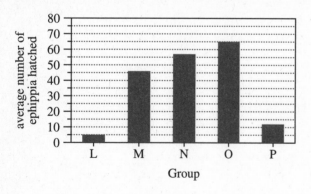

Figure 1

Experiment 2

Each of 20 identical beakers received 50 mL of water and 120 freshly laid *M. micrura* ephippia. The beakers were then equally divided into 5 groups (Groups Q–U). Each beaker was incubated at 25°C, and the water in each beaker was maintained at a pH of 7.0. Group Q was kept in the dark, and each of Groups R–U received 12 hr of light per day at 1 of 4 different light intensities (see Table 2).

Table 2	
Group	Light intensity (lux)
Q	0
R	300
S	650
T	850
U	1,300

At the end of 7 days, the average number of ephippia hatched in each group was determined as in Experiment 1 (see Figure 2).

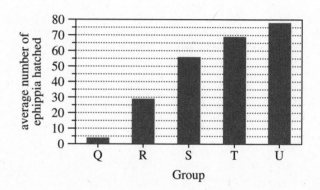

Figure 2

Figures adapted from N. E. T. Rojas, M. A. Marins, and O. Rocha, "The Effect of Abiotic Factors on the Hatching of *Moina micrura* Kurz, 1874 (Crustacea: Cladocera) Ephippial Eggs." ©2001 by the International Institute of Ecology.

14. According to the results of Experiment 2, among the 5 groups tested, as the light intensity increased, the average number of ephippia hatched:

F. decreased only.
G. increased only.
H. decreased and then increased.
J. increased and then decreased.

15. Suppose that a scientist wants to develop an artificial system for hatching *M. micrura* ephippia in a laboratory environment. Based on the results of Experiment 1, which of the pH values tested would most likely maximize the chances of hatching *M. micrura* ephippia in this system?

A. 5.0
B. 7.0
C. 9.0
D. 11.0

GO ON TO THE NEXT PAGE.

4 ○ ○ ○ ○ ○ ○ ○ ○ **4**

16. Consider the units of measurement "mL" and "lux" in Experiment 2. Which of the following phrases best describes the quantities represented by those units?

	mL	lux
F.	mass of water	duration of light exposure
G.	mass of water	light intensity
H.	volume of water	duration of light exposure
J.	volume of water	light intensity

17. Consider the statement "The number of ephippia that hatched, on average, was greater for the ephippia kept in the dark than it was for the ephippia exposed to light." Do the results of Experiment 2 support this statement?

A. Yes; the average number of ephippia hatched in Group R, Group S, Group T, or Group U was greater than the average number of ephippia hatched in Group Q.

B. Yes; the average number of ephippia hatched in Group Q, Group R, Group S, or Group T was greater than the average number of ephippia hatched in Group U.

C. No; the average number of ephippia hatched in Group R, Group S, Group T, or Group U was greater than the average number of ephippia hatched in Group Q.

D. No; the average number of ephippia hatched in Group Q, Group R, Group S, or Group T was greater than the average number of ephippia hatched in Group U.

18. Which of the following pieces of equipment was most likely used to collect the data that were averaged to produce Figures 1 and 2 ?

F. Electronic balance
G. Light microscope
H. Metric ruler
J. pH meter

19. In Experiment 1, the *total* length of time a group of beakers was exposed to light was:

A. 12 hr.
B. 24 hr.
C. 84 hr.
D. 168 hr.

20. Consider the claim "The length of time that the beakers in a group were incubated affected the average number of ephippia hatched in the group." Can this claim be evaluated on the basis of the results of the 2 experiments?

F. Yes, because incubation time was different for each group.
G. Yes, because incubation time was the same for all the groups.
H. No, because incubation time was different for each group.
J. No, because incubation time was the same for all the groups.

GO ON TO THE NEXT PAGE.

4 ○ ○ ○ ○ ○ ○ ○ ○ **4**

Passage IV

Atmospheres (atm), *torr*, and *kilopascals* (kPa) are common units of pressure. Figure 1 can be used to convert between torr and kPa. A pressure of 1 atm is indicated in Figure 1.

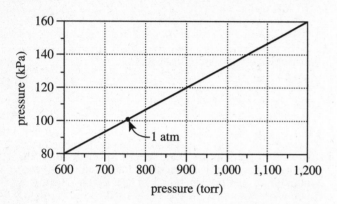

Figure 1

Figure 2 shows how boiling point (*BP*) varies with atmospheric pressure for 3 compounds: acetaldehyde, acetone, and pentane. The unit of pressure is torr.

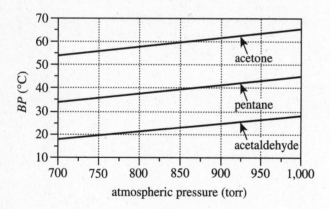

Figure 2

Figure 3 shows how *BP* varies with atmospheric pressure for 3 other compounds: ethanol, methanol, and methyl acetate. The unit of pressure is kPa.

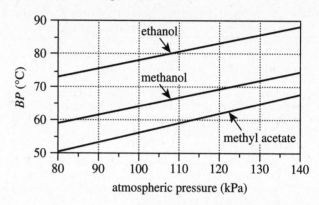

Figure 3

21. According to Figure 2, which of the following graphs best shows the *BP*s of acetaldehyde, acetone, and pentane at 850 torr?

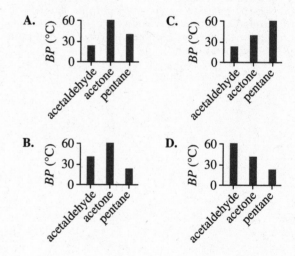

4 ◯ ◯ ◯ ◯ ◯ ◯ ◯ ◯ **4**

22. According to Figure 3, at 110 kPa, the *BP* of methyl acetate is approximately how much lower than or higher than the *BP* of ethanol?

    F. 20°C lower
    G. 10°C lower
    H. 10°C higher
    J. 20°C higher

23. According to Figure 2, the *BP* of pentane at 700 torr is closest to the *BP* of acetaldehyde at which of the following atmospheric pressures?

    A. 700 torr
    B. 800 torr
    C. 900 torr
    D. 1,000 torr

24. A compound's *standard boiling point* is the temperature at which the compound boils when the atmospheric pressure is 1 atm. Based on Figures 1 and 2, the standard boiling point of pentane is approximately:

    F. 21°C.
    G. 36°C.
    H. 57°C.
    J. 66°C.

25. Based on Figure 1, a pressure of 2 atm would correspond to a pressure in torr that is:

    A. less than 700 torr.
    B. between 700 torr and 950 torr.
    C. between 950 torr and 1,200 torr.
    D. greater than 1,200 torr.

26. Suppose a sample of methanol is in a chamber maintained at 60°C and 110 kPa. Based on Figure 3, if the temperature is kept constant, which of the following changes in the pressure will cause the sample to boil?

    F. A decrease of 30 kPa
    G. A decrease of 20 kPa
    H. An increase of 20 kPa
    J. An increase of 30 kPa

GO ON TO THE NEXT PAGE.

4 ○ ○ ○ ○ ○ ○ ○ ○ **4**

Passage V

Multivitamin (MV) tablets often contain iron in the form of Fe^{2+}. In aqueous solution, Fe^{2+} does not absorb visible light. However, when o-phenanthroline (o-phen) is present, it interacts with Fe^{2+} to form an orange-colored complex, which absorbs visible light at a wavelength of 508 nanometers (nm).

Students measured the absorbance at 508 nm—the A_{508}—of 6 solutions having known Fe^{2+} concentrations and then determined the Fe^{2+} content of 4 brands of MV tablets (Brands A–D).

Experiment 1

Steps 1–5 were performed 6 times:

1. A certain volume of an aqueous stock solution having a concentration of 0.04 mg Fe^{2+}/mL was placed in a 100.0 mL flask.

2. Two mL of *hydroquinone* solution was added to the flask to stabilize Fe^{2+}.

3. Three mL of o-phen solution was added to the flask.

4. The contents of the flask were diluted with H_2O to form a solution of 100.0 mL.

5. The A_{508} of the solution formed was measured with a colorimeter.

Table 1 shows, for each of the 6 solutions formed (Solutions 1–6), the volume of stock solution used, the Fe^{2+} concentration, and the A_{508}.

	Table 1		
Solution	Volume of stock solution (mL)	Fe^{2+} concentration (mg/mL)	A_{508}
1	0	0.0000	0.000
2	1	0.0004	0.080
3	2	0.0008	0.159
4	3	0.0012	0.239
5	4	0.0016	0.318
6	5	0.0020	0.398

Experiment 2

Each of Brands A–D was analyzed by crushing 1 tablet, dissolving the powder in H_2O to form a 100.0 mL solution, placing 1 mL of the solution into a flask, and then performing Steps 2–5. From the results, each brand's iron (Fe^{2+}) content, in mg/tablet, was calculated. Table 2 compares, for each brand, the calculated content with the iron (Fe^{2+}) content stated on the label.

	Table 2	
Brand of MV tablet	Stated iron (Fe^{2+}) content (mg/tablet)	Calculated iron (Fe^{2+}) content (mg/tablet)
A	18	16.5
B	8	8.9
C	18	19.1
D	5	5.2

27. Suppose that in Experiment 1, a seventh solution had been formed, beginning with 6 mL of the stock solution. Based on Table 1, if the A_{508} of the seventh solution had been measured, it would most likely have been closest to which of the following?

    A. 0.318
    B. 0.398
    C. 0.480
    D. 0.560

28. Based on Tables 1 and 2, the solution of which brand of MV tablet most likely had the greatest A_{508} value in Experiment 2 ?

    F. Brand A
    G. Brand B
    H. Brand C
    J. Brand D

GO ON TO THE NEXT PAGE.

4 ○ ○ ○ ○ ○ ○ ○ ○ **4**

29. Which of the following graphs best shows the relationship between Fe^{2+} concentration and A_{508} in Experiment 1 ?

A.
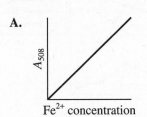
Fe²⁺ concentration

C.
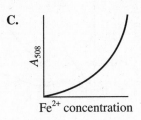
Fe²⁺ concentration

B.
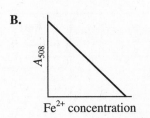
Fe²⁺ concentration

D.
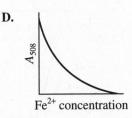
Fe²⁺ concentration

30. Consider the stock solution that was placed in a flask in Step 1. Was this solution more likely orange or colorless?

F. Orange, because it would have absorbed visible light.

G. Orange, because it would not have absorbed visible light.

H. Colorless, because it would have absorbed visible light.

J. Colorless, because it would not have absorbed visible light.

31. In Experiment 1, was the volume of H_2O that had to be added to the flask in Step 4 to form Solution 2 greater than or less than the volume of H_2O that had to be added to the flask in Step 4 to form Solution 5 ?

A. Greater, because the stock solution accounted for a larger volume of Solution 2 than of Solution 5.

B. Greater, because the stock solution accounted for a smaller volume of Solution 2 than of Solution 5.

C. Less, because the stock solution accounted for a smaller volume of Solution 2 than of Solution 5.

D. Less, because the stock solution accounted for a larger volume of Solution 2 than of Solution 5.

32. What was the purpose of Step 3, the addition of o-phen to the flask? The o-phen interacted with:

F. hydroquinone to stabilize Fe^{2+}.

G. hydroquinone to form an orange-colored complex.

H. Fe^{2+} to stabilize hydroquinone.

J. Fe^{2+} to form an orange-colored complex.

33. Experiments 1 and 2 were most likely related to each other in which of the following ways?

A. The A_{508} values of Solutions 1–6 measured in Experiment 1 were used to determine the Fe^{2+} contents of Brands A–D in Experiment 2.

B. The Fe^{2+} contents of Brands A–D calculated in Experiment 2 were used to determine the A_{508} values of Solutions 1–6 in Experiment 1.

C. The A_{508} values of Solutions 1–6 measured in Experiment 2 were used to determine the Fe^{2+} contents of Brands A–D in Experiment 1.

D. The Fe^{2+} contents of Brands A–D calculated in Experiment 1 were used to determine the A_{508} values of Solutions 1–6 in Experiment 2.

GO ON TO THE NEXT PAGE.

4 ◯ ◯ ◯ ◯ ◯ ◯ ◯ **4**

Passage VI

A study was done in a large city in Asia during the spring to examine the composition of airborne dust particles on 5 days of fair weather and on 5 days of dust storms. There was no precipitation on any of the study days.

Study

A device called an *impactor* (see Figure 1) was installed on the roof of a 4-story building in the center of the city. To collect airborne dust particles, the impactor drew in air at a constant rate of 1.1 L/min. A series of 8 filters inside the impactor removed particles from the air. Each filter had openings of a different uniform diameter to allow for the collection of particles belonging to 1 of 8 different size ranges, measured in micrometers (μm).

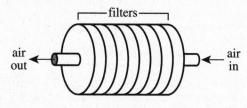

Figure 1

On each of the selected days, the impactor was operated continuously over a period that began at 9 a.m. At 3 p.m., the impactor was turned off, and the collected particles belonging to each size range were removed and then analyzed for 4 elements: silicon (Si), iron (Fe), sulfur (S), and copper (Cu). The average concentration of each element, in micrograms per cubic meter of air (μg/m³), for the fair weather days and for the dust storm days are shown in Figures 2 and 3, respectively, for each size range.

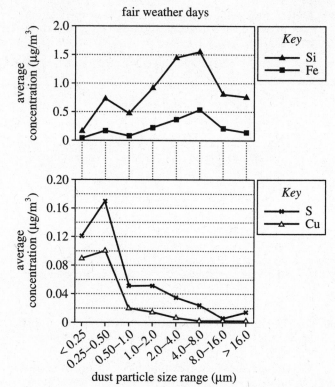

Figure 2

GO ON TO THE NEXT PAGE.

4 ◯ ◯ ◯ ◯ ◯ ◯ ◯ ◯ 4

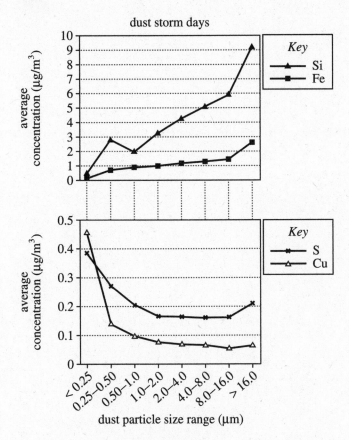

dust storm days

Figure 3

Figures 2 and 3 adapted from Renjian Zhang et al., "The Elemental Composition of Atmospheric Particles at Beijing during Asian Dust Events in Spring 2004." ©2010 by the Taiwan Association for Aerosol Research.

34. Consider the results of the study for the dust storm days. Did the larger dust particles (> 2.0 μm) or the smaller dust particles (< 2.0 μm) have the greater average concentrations of Si and Fe, and did the larger dust particles or the smaller dust particles have the greater average concentrations of S and Cu ?

	greater Si and Fe	greater S and Cu
F.	larger dust particles	larger dust particles
G.	larger dust particles	smaller dust particles
H.	smaller dust particles	larger dust particles
J.	smaller dust particles	smaller dust particles

35. The total volume of air, in liters, that was drawn through the impactor each hour is given by which of the following expressions?

   A. 1.1 L/min × 60 min
   B. 1.1 L/min ÷ 60 min
   C. 1.1 L/min × 1 hr
   D. 1.1 L/min ÷ 1 hr

36. Days with no precipitation were most likely chosen as study days because precipitation would have:

   F. caused dust particles in the air to condense.
   G. caused dust particles in the air to vaporize.
   H. removed dust particles from the air.
   J. put more dust particles into the air.

37. What was the average mass of the < 0.25 μm dust particles that were collected by the impactor on the fair weather days?

   A.   0.5 μg
   B.   5 μg
   C.   50 μg
   D. Cannot be determined from the given information

38. For both the fair weather days and the dust storm days, why were the results for Si and Fe plotted on a different *y*-axis scale than were the results for S and Cu ?

   F. In general, Si and Fe were present at much lesser concentrations in the particles than were S and Cu.
   G. In general, Si and Fe were present at much greater concentrations in the particles than were S and Cu.
   H. Particles containing Si and Fe belonged to smaller particle size ranges than did particles containing S and Cu.
   J. Particles containing Si and Fe belonged to larger particle size ranges than did particles containing S and Cu.

39. The average concentrations of how many of the elements were generally greater for the dust storm days than for the fair weather days?

   A. 1
   B. 2
   C. 3
   D. 4

40. Based on the description of the design of the impactor, particles belonging to which size range were removed from the air by the first filter the air passed through?

   F. < 0.25 μm
   G. 0.50–1.0 μm
   H. 2.0–4.0 μm
   J. > 16.0 μm

END OF TEST 4

STOP! DO NOT RETURN TO ANY OTHER TEST.

You may wish to photocopy these sample answer document pages to respond to the practice ACT Writing Test.

Please enter the information at the right before beginning the writing test.

Use a soft lead No. 2 pencil only. Do NOT use a mechanical pencil, ink, ballpoint, or felt-tip pen.

WRITING TEST BOOKLET NUMBER

Print your 6-digit **Booklet Number** in the boxes at the right.

WRITING TEST FORM

◯ 20WT7

Print your 5-character **Test Form** in the boxes above <u>and</u> fill in the corresponding oval at the right.

Begin WRITING TEST here.

If you need more space, please continue on the next page.

1

WRITING TEST

_____

_____

_____

_____

_____

_____

_____

_____

_____

_____

_____

_____

_____

_____

_____

_____

_____

_____

_____

_____

_____

_____

_____

_____

_____

_____

_____

If you need more space, please continue on the back of this page.

WRITING TEST

_____

_____

_____

_____

_____

_____

_____

_____

_____

_____

_____

_____

_____

_____

_____

_____

_____

_____

_____

_____

_____

_____

If you need more space, please continue on the next page.

3

WRITING TEST

_____

_____

_____

_____

_____

_____

_____

_____

_____

_____

_____

_____

_____

_____

_____

_____

_____

_____

_____

_____

_____

_____

_____

_____

_____

_____

_____

_____

_____

_____

STOP here with the writing test.

193055   # Practice Writing Test

Your Signature: _____
(Do not print.)

Print Your Name Here: _____

Your Date of Birth:

		–			–				
Month		Day			Year				

Form 20WT7

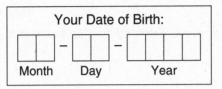 WRITING TEST
BOOKLET

You must take the multiple-choice tests before you take the writing test.

Directions

This is a test of your writing skills. You will have **forty** (40) minutes to read the prompt, plan your response, and write an essay in English. Before you begin working, read all material in this test booklet carefully to understand exactly what you are being asked to do.

You will write your essay on the lined pages in the **answer document** provided. Your writing on those pages will be scored. You may use the unlined pages in this test booklet to plan your essay. Your work on these pages will not be scored.

Your essay will be evaluated based on the evidence it provides of your ability to:

- clearly state your own perspective on a complex issue and analyze the relationship between your perspective and at least one other perspective
- develop and support your ideas with reasoning and examples
- organize your ideas clearly and logically
- communicate your ideas effectively in standard written English

Lay your pencil down immediately when time is called.

DO NOT OPEN THIS BOOKLET UNTIL TOLD TO DO SO.

 PO Box 168
Iowa City, IA 52243-0168

The Same Old Story

People spend a lot of time and money on entertainment. Excited audiences take in the latest movies, television shows, and books and then eagerly await the next ones. But much of this entertainment seems to be based on recycled story lines: good triumphs over evil, opposites attract and find true love, the awkward misfit saves the world. Many of the characters are also the same: the wise old mentor, the reluctant hero, the funny best friend. Why do people spend time and money on stories based on recycled characters and plots?

Read and carefully consider these perspectives. Each suggests a particular way of thinking about the question above.

Perspective One	Perspective Two	Perspective Three
Real life is unpredictable; we can't ever be sure how things will turn out. We seek out the same old stories in our entertainment because we find comfort in knowing how they will end—that goodness and love will win.	Most people want entertainment, not a challenge. Familiar stories and characters are easy for people to enjoy without having to think very hard.	We find these stories appealing because they contain universal truths. Each retelling uses changes in conflict, character, and setting to help us better understand important ideas about the world.

Essay Task

Write a unified, coherent essay in which you address the question of why people spend time and money on stories based on recycled characters and plots. In your essay, be sure to:

- clearly state your own perspective and analyze the relationship between your perspective and at least one other perspective
- develop and support your ideas with reasoning and examples
- organize your ideas clearly and logically
- communicate your ideas effectively in standard written English

Your perspective may be in full agreement with any of those given, in partial agreement, or completely different.

Planning Your Essay

Your work on these prewriting pages will not be scored.

Use the space below and on the back cover to generate ideas and plan your essay. You may wish to consider the following as you think critically about the task:

Strengths and weaknesses of different perspectives on the issue
- What insights do they offer, and what do they fail to consider?
- Why might they be persuasive to others, or why might they fail to persuade?

Your own knowledge, experience, and values
- What is your perspective on this issue, and what are its strengths and weaknesses?
- How will you support your perspective in your essay?

If you need more space to plan, please continue on the back of this page.

Planning Your Essay

Use this page to continue planning your essay. Your work on this page will not be scored.

Chapter 4: Scoring Your Practice Test

After taking the practice test in this book, you are ready to score the test to see how you did. In this chapter, you learn how to determine your raw score, convert raw scores to scale scores, compute your Composite score, determine your estimated percentile ranks for each of your scale scores, and score your practice writing test essay. There is also an option to take the multiple-choice section only online. In this case there will be no need to use this scoring section for the multiple-choice section as your score will be provided to you automatically. If you take the multiple-choice section online, please use the paper test for the Writing section and the information in this chapter to score your essay.

When scoring the practice test and reviewing your scores, remember that your scores on the practice test are only estimates of the scores that you will obtain on the ACT. If your score isn't as high as you expected, the cause could be related to any number of factors. Maybe you need to review important content and skills. Maybe you should work a little faster, or more slowly and carefully, when taking the test. Perhaps you simply weren't doing your best work on the test. Or maybe you need to take more challenging courses to be better prepared. Keep in mind that a test score is just one indicator of your level of academic knowledge and skills. You know your own strengths and weaknesses better than anyone else, so keep them in mind as you evaluate your performance.

Scoring Your Practice Test

For the multiple-choice tests (English, mathematics, reading, and science), the number of questions you answer correctly is called a *raw* score. To figure out your raw scores from your practice test, count the number of correct answers from each multiple-choice test using the scoring keys provided in the following sections. Then you can convert your raw scores into *scale* scores. Scale scores are the scores that ACT reports to students, high schools, colleges, and scholarship agencies. Raw scores are converted to a common scale score to enhance score interpretation and allow comparability across different forms. After you've converted your raw scores for the practice test to scale scores, you'll want to convert your scale scores to percentile ranks. Percentile ranks, which are explained in the following pages, are useful for interpreting your score relative to the scores of others who have taken the ACT.

If you took the optional practice writing test, use the analytic rubric on pages 104–105 to evaluate your essay and estimate your writing test score. Being objective about one's own work is difficult, and you have not had the extensive training provided to actual readers of the ACT writing test. However, it is to your advantage to read your own writing critically. Becoming your own editor helps you grow as a writer and as a reader, so it makes sense for you to evaluate your own practice essay. That having been said, it may also be helpful for you to give your practice essay to another reader to get another perspective: perhaps that of a classmate, a parent, or an English teacher, for example. To rate your essay, you and your reader should be familiar with the analytic rubric on pages 104–105, and then assign your practice essay a score of 1 (low) through 6 (high) in each of the four writing domains (Ideas and Analysis, Development and Support, Organization, and Language Use and Conventions).

Your writing test should be based on two ratings, so you may either multiply your own rating times two, or sum your rating and another reader's rating to calculate your domain scores (2–12 for each domain). Your raw score is the average of your domain scores and will be in a range of 2–12.

Scoring Your Multiple-Choice Tests

To score each of your multiple-choice practice tests, starting with the English test, follow these six steps:

STEP 1. Write a "1" in the blank for each question that you answered correctly. An example is provided in the following box:

	Key		Your answer was
1.	A	–	Incorrect
2.	J	1	Correct
3.	B	1	Correct
4.	G	–	Incorrect

English ■ Scoring Key ■ Practice Test 20MC7

	Key			Key			Key	
1.	C	_____	26.	G	_____	51.	B	_____
2.	F	_____	27.	C	_____	52.	J	_____
3.	B	_____	28.	J	_____	53.	C	_____
4.	G	_____	29.	A	_____	54.	F	_____
5.	B	_____	30.	J	_____	55.	B	_____
6.	H	_____	31.	D	_____	56.	F	_____
7.	A	_____	32.	G	_____	57.	C	_____
8.	J	_____	33.	A	_____	58.	J	_____
9.	A	_____	34.	H	_____	59.	C	_____
10.	H	_____	35.	C	_____	60.	H	_____
11.	D	_____	36.	G	_____	61.	B	_____
12.	H	_____	37.	C	_____	62.	H	_____
13.	B	_____	38.	F	_____	63.	C	_____
14.	J	_____	39.	C	_____	64.	J	_____
15.	C	_____	40.	F	_____	65.	D	_____
16.	F	_____	41.	B	_____	66.	H	_____
17.	B	_____	42.	J	_____	67.	A	_____
18.	J	_____	43.	D	_____	68.	J	_____
19.	C	_____	44.	F	_____	69.	C	_____
20.	J	_____	45.	C	_____	70.	F	_____
21.	B	_____	46.	G	_____	71.	A	_____
22.	J	_____	47.	A	_____	72.	J	_____
23.	A	_____	48.	F	_____	73.	A	_____
24.	G	_____	49.	D	_____	74.	G	_____
25.	B	_____	50.	J	_____	75.	B	_____

STEP 2. Add the numbers you entered in Step 1 and write this total in the following shaded box. This is your raw score.

Number Correct (Raw Score) for:	
English Test (75 questions)	_____

STEP 3. Repeat Steps 1 and 2 for the ACT mathematics, reading, and science tests using the scoring keys on the following pages.

Mathematics ■ Scoring Key ■ Practice Test 20MC7

	Key			Key			Key	
1.	A	_____	21.	A	_____	41.	B	_____
2.	J	_____	22.	J	_____	42.	F	_____
3.	C	_____	23.	A	_____	43.	C	_____
4.	K	_____	24.	G	_____	44.	F	_____
5.	C	_____	25.	C	_____	45.	A	_____
6.	H	_____	26.	H	_____	46.	H	_____
7.	A	_____	27.	C	_____	47.	B	_____
8.	G	_____	28.	H	_____	48.	K	_____
9.	E	_____	29.	D	_____	49.	E	_____
10.	G	_____	30.	G	_____	50.	H	_____
11.	D	_____	31.	D	_____	51.	D	_____
12.	G	_____	32.	H	_____	52.	J	_____
13.	B	_____	33.	A	_____	53.	B	_____
14.	J	_____	34.	F	_____	54.	J	_____
15.	E	_____	35.	B	_____	55.	D	_____
16.	K	_____	36.	G	_____	56.	F	_____
17.	E	_____	37.	E	_____	57.	A	_____
18.	J	_____	38.	J	_____	58.	F	_____
19.	A	_____	39.	D	_____	59.	E	_____
20.	G	_____	40.	K	_____	60.	K	_____

Number Correct (Raw Score) for:	
Total Number Correct for Math Test (60 questions)	_____

Reading ■ Scoring Key ■ Practice Test 20MC7

	Key			Key			Key	
1.	D	_____	15.	B	_____	29.	A	_____
2.	H	_____	16.	F	_____	30.	G	_____
3.	B	_____	17.	C	_____	31.	D	_____
4.	H	_____	18.	G	_____	32.	F	_____
5.	A	_____	19.	D	_____	33.	B	_____
6.	J	_____	20.	F	_____	34.	G	_____
7.	B	_____	21.	C	_____	35.	C	_____
8.	J	_____	22.	H	_____	36.	J	_____
9.	D	_____	23.	D	_____	37.	A	_____
10.	H	_____	24.	F	_____	38.	H	_____
11.	C	_____	25.	D	_____	39.	C	_____
12.	G	_____	26.	F	_____	40.	G	_____
13.	C	_____	27.	C	_____			
14.	J	_____	28.	G	_____			

Number Correct (Raw Score) for:

Reading Test (40 questions)   _____

Science ■ Scoring Key ■ Practice Test 20MC7

	Key			Key			Key	
1.	C	_____	15.	C	_____	29.	A	_____
2.	F	_____	16.	J	_____	30.	J	_____
3.	B	_____	17.	C	_____	31.	B	_____
4.	J	_____	18.	G	_____	32.	J	_____
5.	C	_____	19.	C	_____	33.	A	_____
6.	H	_____	20.	J	_____	34.	G	_____
7.	A	_____	21.	A	_____	35.	A	_____
8.	F	_____	22.	F	_____	36.	H	_____
9.	A	_____	23.	D	_____	37.	D	_____
10.	H	_____	24.	G	_____	38.	G	_____
11.	D	_____	25.	D	_____	39.	D	_____
12.	F	_____	26.	F	_____	40.	J	_____
13.	B	_____	27.	C	_____			
14.	G	_____	28.	H	_____			

Number Correct (Raw Score) for:

Science Test (40 questions)   _____

STEP 4. On each of the four tests, the total number of correct responses yields a raw score. Use the conversion table on the following page to convert your raw scores to scale scores. For each of the four tests, locate and circle your raw score or the range of raw scores that includes it in the conversion table. Then, read across to either outside column of the table and circle the scale score that corresponds to that raw score. As you determine your scale scores, enter them in the blanks provided below. The highest possible scale score for each test is 36. The lowest possible scale score for any of the four tests is 1.

	Your Scale Scores
English	_____
Mathematics	_____
Reading	_____
Science	_____
Sum of Scores	_____

STEP 5. Compute your Composite score by averaging the four scale scores. To do this, add your four scale scores and divide the sum by 4. If the resulting number ends in a fraction, round it off to the nearest whole number. (Round down any fraction less than one-half; round up any fraction that is one-half or more.) Enter this number in the appropriate blank below. This is your Composite score. The highest possible Composite score is 36. The lowest possible Composite score is 1.

	Your Scale Scores
English	_____
Mathematics	_____
Reading	_____
Science	_____
Sum of Scores	_____
Composite Score (sum ÷ 4)	_____

Scale Score Conversion Table: Practice Test 20MC7

Scale Score	Raw Score				Scale Score
	English	Mathematics	Reading	Science	
36	74–75	59–60	39–40	40	36
35	71–73	57–58	38	39	35
34	70	56	37	38	34
33	69	54–55	36	37	33
32	–	53	35	–	32
31	68	51–52	34	36	31
30	66–67	50	33	35	30
29	65	48–49	32	34	29
28	64	45–47	31	33	28
27	62–63	42–44	–	32	27
26	61	39–41	30	31	26
25	58–60	36–38	29	30	25
24	55–57	33–35	27–28	28–29	24
23	52–54	31–32	26	26–27	23
22	49–51	29–30	24–25	24–25	22
21	47–48	28	23	22–23	21
20	44–46	26–27	22	20–21	20
19	42–43	24–25	20–21	19	19
18	40–41	21–23	19	17–18	18
17	38–39	18–20	17–18	15–16	17
16	35–37	15–17	16	14	16
15	31–34	12–14	15	12–13	15
14	28–30	9–11	13–14	11	14
13	26–27	7–8	12	10	13
12	23–25	5–6	10–11	9	12
11	20–22	4	9	8	11
10	17–19	–	7–8	7	10
9	15–16	3	6	6	9
8	12–14	–	5	5	8
7	10–11	2	–	4	7
6	8–9	–	4	3	6
5	6–7	1	3	–	5
4	5	–	2	2	4
3	3–4	–	–	1	3
2	2	–	1	–	2
1	0–1	0	0	0	1

STEP 6. Use the table on page 102 to determine your estimated percentile ranks (percent at or below) for each of your scale scores. In the far left column of the table, circle your scale score for the English test (from page 100). Then read across to the percentile rank column for that test; circle or put a checkmark beside the corresponding percentile rank. Use the same procedure for the other three tests (from page 100). Using the right-hand column of scale scores for your science test and Composite scores may be easier. As you mark your percentile ranks, enter them in the blanks provided. You may also find it helpful to compare your performance with the national mean (average) score for each of the four tests and the Composite as shown at the bottom of the table.

National Distributions of Cumulative Percents for ACT Test Scores
ACT-Tested High School Graduates from 2016, 2017, and 2018

Score	ENGLISH	MATHEMATICS	READING	SCIENCE	COMPOSITE	STEM	Score
36	100	100	100	100	100	100	36
35	99	99	99	99	99	99	35
34	97	99	97	99	99	99	34
33	95	98	95	97	98	98	33
32	93	97	93	96	97	97	32
31	92	96	90	95	95	96	31
30	91	95	88	94	93	94	30
29	88	93	85	92	91	93	29
28	87	91	83	91	89	91	28
27	85	88	80	88	86	88	27
26	82	83	77	86	82	84	26
25	79	79	74	82	78	80	25
24	75	74	71	77	74	75	24
23	70	68	66	70	69	69	23
22	64	64	60	64	63	64	22
21	59	60	54	56	58	58	21
20	53	56	48	49	51	52	20
19	47	52	43	42	45	45	19
18	43	47	37	36	39	38	18
17	39	40	31	29	32	30	17
16	35	30	27	23	26	23	16
15	29	18	22	17	20	15	15
14	23	9	17	13	14	9	14
13	18	3	12	9	8	4	13
12	14	1	8	6	4	2	12
11	10	1	4	4	1	1	11
10	6	1	2	2	1	1	10
9	3	1	1	1	1	1	9
8	2	1	1	1	1	1	8
7	1	1	1	1	1	1	7
6	1	1	1	1	1	1	6
5	1	1	1	1	1	1	5
4	1	1	1	1	1	1	4
3	1	1	1	1	1	1	3
2	1	1	1	1	1	1	2
1	1	1	1	1	1	1	1
Mean	20.2	20.6	21.3	20.8	20.9	20.9	
S.D.	6.9	5.5	6.6	5.6	5.7	5.3	

Note: These national norms are the source of U.S. ranks, for multiple-choice tests, displayed on ACT reports during the 2018-2019 testing year.

These norms with a sample size of 6,035,197, are based on 2016, 2017, and 2018 graduates.

Scoring Your Practice Writing Test Essay

To score your practice writing test essay, follow these steps:

STEP 1. Use the guidelines on the following analytic rubric to score your essay. Because many essays do not fit the exact description at each score point, read each description and try to determine which paragraph in the rubric best describes most of the characteristics of your essay.

The ACT Writing Test Analytic Rubric

	Ideas and Analysis	Development and Support	Organization	Language Use and Conventions
Score 6: **Responses at this scorepoint demonstrate effective skill in writing an argumentative essay.**	The writer generates an argument that critically engages with multiple perspectives on the given issue. The argument's thesis reflects nuance and precision in thought and purpose. The argument establishes and employs an insightful context for analysis of the issue and its perspectives. The analysis examines implications, complexities and tensions, and/or underlying values and assumptions.	Development of ideas and support for claims deepen insight and broaden context. An integrated line of skillful reasoning and illustration effectively conveys the significance of the argument. Qualifications and complications enrich and bolster ideas and analysis.	The response exhibits a skillful organizational strategy. The response is unified by a controlling idea or purpose, and a logical progression of ideas increases the effectiveness of the writer's argument. Transitions between and within paragraphs strengthen the relationships among ideas.	The use of language enhances the argument. Word choice is skillful and precise. Sentence structures are consistently varied and clear. Stylistic and register choices, including voice and tone, are strategic and effective. While a few minor errors in grammar, usage, and mechanics may be present, they do not impede understanding.
Score 5: **Responses at this scorepoint demonstrate well-developed skill in writing an argumentative essay.**	The writer generates an argument that productively engages with multiple perspectives on the given issue. The argument's thesis reflects precision in thought and purpose. The argument establishes and employs a thoughtful context for analysis of the issue and its perspectives. The analysis addresses implications, complexities and tensions, and/or underlying values and assumptions.	Development of ideas and support for claims deepen understanding. A mostly integrated line of purposeful reasoning and illustration capably conveys the significance of the argument. Qualifications and complications enrich ideas and analysis.	The response exhibits a productive organizational strategy. The response is mostly unified by a controlling idea or purpose, and a logical sequencing of ideas contributes to the effectiveness of the argument. Transitions between and within paragraphs consistently clarify the relationships among ideas.	The use of language works in service of the argument. Word choice is precise. Sentence structures are clear and varied often. Stylistic and register choices, including voice and tone, are purposeful and productive. While minor errors in grammar, usage, and mechanics may be present, they do not impede understanding.
Score 4: **Responses at this scorepoint demonstrate adequate skill in writing an argumentative essay.**	The writer generates an argument that engages with multiple perspectives on the given issue. The argument's thesis reflects clarity in thought and purpose. The argument establishes and employs a relevant context for analysis of the issue and its perspectives. The analysis recognizes implications, complexities and tensions, and/or underlying values and assumptions.	Development of ideas and support for claims clarify meaning and purpose. Lines of clear reasoning and illustration adequately convey the significance of the argument. Qualifications and complications extend ideas and analysis.	The response exhibits a clear organizational strategy. The overall shape of the response reflects an emergent controlling idea or purpose. Ideas are logically grouped and sequenced. Transitions between and within paragraphs clarify the relationships among ideas.	The use of language conveys the argument with clarity. Word choice is adequate and sometimes precise. Sentence structures are clear and demonstrate some variety. Stylistic and register choices, including voice and tone, are appropriate for the rhetorical purpose. While errors in grammar, usage, and mechanics are present, they rarely impede understanding.
Score 3: **Responses at this scorepoint demonstrate some developing skill in writing an argumentative essay.**	The writer generates an argument that responds to multiple perspectives on the given issue. The argument's thesis reflects some clarity in thought and purpose. The argument establishes a limited or tangential context for analysis of the issue and its perspectives. Analysis is simplistic or somewhat unclear.	Development of ideas and support for claims are mostly relevant but are overly general or simplistic. Reasoning and illustration largely clarify the argument but may be somewhat repetitious or imprecise.	The response exhibits a basic organizational structure. The response largely coheres, with most ideas logically grouped. Transitions between and within paragraphs sometimes clarify the relationships among ideas.	The use of language is basic and only somewhat clear. Word choice is general and occasionally imprecise. Sentence structures are usually clear but show little variety. Stylistic and register choices, including voice and tone, are not always appropriate for the rhetorical purpose. Distracting errors in grammar, usage, and mechanics may be present, but they generally do not impede understanding.

(continued)

The ACT Writing Test Analytic Rubric

	Ideas and Analysis	Development and Support	Organization	Language Use and Conventions
Score 2: **Responses at this scorepoint demonstrate weak or inconsistent skill in writing an argumentative essay.**	The writer generates an argument that weakly responds to multiple perspectives on the given issue. The argument's thesis, if evident, reflects little clarity in thought and purpose. Attempts at analysis are incomplete, largely irrelevant, or consist primarily of restatement of the issue and its perspectives.	Development of ideas and support for claims are weak, confused, or disjointed. Reasoning and illustration are inadequate, illogical, or circular, and fail to fully clarify the argument.	The response exhibits a rudimentary organizational structure. Grouping of ideas is inconsistent and often unclear. Transitions between and within paragraphs are misleading or poorly formed.	The use of language is inconsistent and often unclear. Word choice is rudimentary and frequently imprecise. Sentence structures are sometimes unclear. Stylistic and register choices, including voice and tone, are inconsistent and are not always appropriate for the rhetorical purpose. Distracting errors in grammar, usage, and mechanics are present, and they sometimes impede understanding.
Score 1: **Responses at this scorepoint demonstrate little or no skill in writing an argumentative essay.**	The writer fails to generate an argument that responds intelligibly to the task. The writer's intentions are difficult to discern. Attempts at analysis are unclear or irrelevant.	Ideas lack development, and claims lack support. Reasoning and illustration are unclear, incoherent, or largely absent.	The response does not exhibit an organizational structure. There is little grouping of ideas. When present, transitional devices fail to connect ideas.	The use of language fails to demonstrate skill in responding to the task. Word choice is imprecise and often difficult to comprehend. Sentence structures are often unclear. Stylistic and register choices are difficult to identify. Errors in grammar, usage, and mechanics are pervasive and often impede understanding.

STEP 2. Because your writing test domain scores are the sum of two readers' ratings of your essay, multiply your own 1–6 rating from step 1 by 2. Or, have both you and someone else read and score your practice essay, add those ratings together, and record the total in the Domain Score column in step 3.

STEP 3. Enter your writing test domain scores in the following box.

		Domain Score
Ideas and Analysis	_____ × 2 =	_____
Development and Support	_____ × 2 =	_____
Organization	_____ × 2 =	_____
Language Use and Conventions	_____ × 2 =	_____

STEP 4. Enter the sum of the second-column scores here _____.

STEP 5. Divide sum by 4† (range 2–12). This is your Writing Subject score.

†Round value to the nearest whole number. Round down any fraction less than one-half; round up any fraction that is one-half or more.

STEP 6. Use the table on page 107 to determine your estimated percentile rank (percent at or below) for your writing subject score.

National Distributions of Cumulative Percents
Writing Score

ACT-Tested High School Graduates
from 2016, 2017, and 2018

Score	Writing
12	22
11	18
10	15
9	12
8	7
7	5
6	4
5	3
4	3
3	2
2	2
1	1
Mean	17.8
S.D.	6.4

Note: The norms for the ACT ELA and 2–12 Writing scores are the source of U.S. and state ranks printed on ACT score reports during the 2018–2019 testing year. The norms for the ACT 1–36 Writing scores are the source of U.S. and state ranks printed on ACT supplemental score reports for test events between September 2015 and June 2017.
These norms with a sample size of 2,839,108, are based on 2016, 2017, and 2018 graduates.

Chapter 5:
Interpreting Your ACT Test Scores and Ranks

After taking any test, students are eager to see how they've done. Because you have taken an ACT practice test, you now have information to consider when determining how well you did.

- **Raw scores:** ACT does not provide raw scores, but you have raw scores for the practice test in this book.

- **Scale scores** are the scores that ACT reports to students, high schools, colleges, and scholarship agencies.

- **Composite score** is a scale score that reflects your overall performance on *all* of the multiple choice tests—English, math, reading, and science.

- **Ranks** indicate the approximate percentage of ACT-tested students who scored at or below each of your scores; for example, if your mathematics rank is 85%, then you scored as well or better than 85% of the other students who took the mathematics test.

If you take the ACT you receive the *ACT Student Report*, which includes scale scores, the Composite score, and the rank for each score. You can visit www.act.org to view samples of this report as well as the High School and College reports.

ANN C TAYLOR (ACT ID: -54116290)
WHEAT RIDGE SR HIGH SCHOOL (061-450)
TEST DATE: APRIL 2019

Student Report

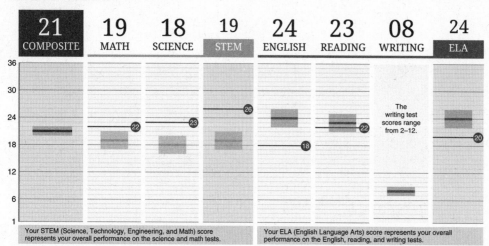

21	19	18	19	24	23	08	24
COMPOSITE	MATH	SCIENCE	STEM	ENGLISH	READING	WRITING	ELA

Your STEM (Science, Technology, Engineering, and Math) score represents your overall performance on the science and math tests.

Your ELA (English Language Arts) score represents your overall performance on the English, reading, and writing tests.

The writing test scores range from 2–12.

Your Score

━━━ Your Score

▭ Your Score Range

ACT College Readiness Benchmarks

⬤━ Readiness Benchmark

If your score is at or above the Benchmark, you have at least a 50% chance of obtaining a B or higher or about a 75% chance of obtaining a C or higher in specific first-year college courses in the corresponding subject area. There is currently no Benchmark for writing.

Your Score Range

Test scores are estimates of your educational development. Think of your true achievement on this test as being within a range that extends about one standard error of measurement, or about 1 point for the Composite and writing scores, and 2 points for STEM, ELA, and the other test scores, above and below your score.

US & State Rank

Your ranks tell you the approximate percentages of recent high school graduates in the US and your state who took the ACT® test and received scores that are the same as or lower than your scores. For example, a rank of 56 for your Composite score means 56% of students earned that Composite score or below.

US Rank

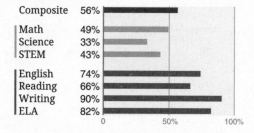

Composite	56%
Math	49%
Science	33%
STEM	43%
English	74%
Reading	66%
Writing	90%
ELA	82%

State Rank

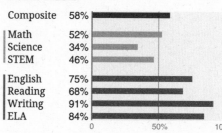

Composite	58%
Math	52%
Science	34%
STEM	46%
English	75%
Reading	68%
Writing	91%
ELA	84%

Detailed Results

MATH   19

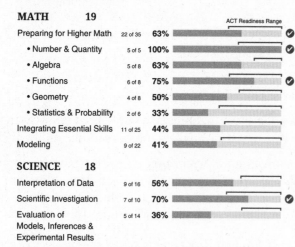

			ACT Readiness Range
Preparing for Higher Math	22 of 35	63%	✓
• Number & Quantity	5 of 5	100%	✓
• Algebra	5 of 8	63%	✓
• Functions	6 of 8	75%	✓
• Geometry	4 of 8	50%	
• Statistics & Probability	2 of 6	33%	
Integrating Essential Skills	11 of 25	44%	
Modeling	9 of 22	41%	

SCIENCE   18

Interpretation of Data	9 of 16	56%	
Scientific Investigation	7 of 10	70%	✓
Evaluation of Models, Inferences & Experimental Results	5 of 14	36%	

ACT Composite Score: ACT math, science, English, and reading test scores and the Composite score range from 1 to 36. For each test, we converted your number of correct answers into a score within that range. Your Composite score is the average of your scores on the four subjects rounded to the nearest whole number. If you left any test completely blank, that score is reported as two dashes and no Composite score is computed.

ACT Readiness Range: This range shows where a student who has met the ACT College Readiness Benchmark on this subject test would typically perform.

ENGLISH   24

			ACT Readiness Range
Production of Writing	16 of 23	70%	✓
Knowledge of Language	8 of 12	67%	✓
Conventions of Standard English	29 of 40	73%	✓

READING   23

Key Ideas & Details	18 of 24	75%	✓
Craft & Structure	6 of 11	55%	
Integration of Knowledge & Ideas	3 of 5	60%	✓
Understanding Complex Texts			

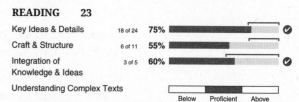

Below   Proficient   Above

Understanding Complex Texts: This indicator lets you know if you are understanding the central meaning of complex texts at a level that is needed to succeed in college courses with higher reading demand.

WRITING   08

Ideas & Analysis	8
Development & Support	8
Organization	9
Language Use & Conventions	8

If you took the writing test, your essay was scored on a scale of 1 to 6 by two raters in each of the four writing domains. These domains represent essential skills and abilities that are necessary to meet the writing demands of college and career. Your domain scores, ranging from 2 to 12, are a sum of the two raters' scores. Your writing score is the average of your four domain scores rounded to the nearest whole number. To learn more about your writing score, visit **www.act.org/the-act/writing-scores**.

Dashes (-) indicate information was not provided or could not be calculated.

In this chapter, we explain how to interpret your scores and use them as a tool to help inform your education and career decisions. We encourage you to look at your ACT test scores and ranks with additional information to help guide your future education and career planning.

Understanding Your ACT Test Results

Your scores, Composite score, and ranks provide a good indication of how well you did on the test, but you can interpret these scores on a deeper level to find out more about how well prepared you are to tackle a certain course of studies or pursue a specific career. In the following sections, we help you put your scores and ranks in perspective to make them more meaningful and relevant to your education and career planning.

How ACT Scores Your Multiple-Choice Tests

ACT scores the multiple-choice tests the same way you scored your ACT practice test in chapter 4. The first step is to do exactly what you did for your practice test: count the number of questions you answered correctly to determine your raw score. No points are deducted for incorrect answers.

The raw score is converted to a scale score to enhance score interpretation and allow comparability across different forms. Scale scores range from 1 (low) to 36 (high) for each of the four individual tests and for the Composite score, which is the average of the four test scores.

How ACT Scores Your Writing Test

Two trained readers score each writing test based on the analytic rubric presented on pages 104–105. Each reader scores your essay on a scale from 1 (low) to 6 (high) on each domain. If their scores differ by more than 1 point on any of the four domains, a third reader scores your essay to resolve the discrepancy. This method is designed to be as impartial as possible. The writing score is calculated from your domain scores and is reported on a 2-to-12 scale.

Recognizing That Test Scores Are Estimates of Educational Achievement

No test, including the ACT, is an exact measure of your educational achievement. We estimate the amount of imprecision using the "standard error of measurement." On the ACT, the standard error of measurement (SEM) is 2 points for each of the multiple-choice tests, 4 points for the writing test, and 1 point for the Composite score.

Because no test score is an exact measure of your achievement, think of each of your ACT scores as a range of scores rather than as a precise number. The SEM can be used to estimate ranges for your scores. To do this, just add the SEM to, and subtract it from, each of your scores. For example, if your score on the English test is 22, your true achievement is likely in the score range of 20 to 24 (22 plus or minus 2 points). Beginning with the September 2020 national test date, students who have taken the ACT test more than once will have a Super Composite score (superscore) calculated on their behalf by ACT. Superscoring allows students to utilize their highest individual section scores across all of their test events for ACT to calculate the best possible Composite score. These test events could be from a student taking the full ACT test or from a section retest event. Students will have the option to send an individual full battery Composite score or a superscore to colleges or scholarship agencies.

Using Ranks to Interpret Your Scores

The US and state ranks for a score tell you how your scores compare to those earned by recent high school graduates who took the ACT. The numbers indicate the cumulative percent of students who scored at or below a given score. For example, if your rank is 63%, then 63% of recent high school graduates who took the ACT scored at or below your score.

Comparing Your Test Scores to Each Other

Another way to interpret your ACT test scores is by comparing them to each other using the ranks. You may find it interesting, for example, to compare your ranks for the science and mathematics tests to your ranks for the reading and English tests. Perhaps you felt more comfortable and successful in some subject areas than in others. Making comparisons among your ACT test ranks can be especially helpful as you make decisions about the courses you will take in high school and college. A high rank in a particular area indicates that you compare well to other ACT test-takers in that subject. A low rank may indicate that you need to develop your skills more in that area.

Keep in mind, however, that scale scores from the different individual tests can't be directly compared to each other. Scoring 23 on the ACT English and mathematics tests, for example, doesn't necessarily mean that your levels of skill and knowledge in English are the same as they are in mathematics. The percentile ranks corresponding to the scores—not the scores themselves—are probably best for making comparisons among subject areas.

Comparing Your Scores and Ranks to Your High School Grades

After you take the ACT and receive your student report, compare your scores and ranks to your high school grades. Are your highest grades and highest ACT test scores and ranks in the same content areas? If so, you might want to consider college majors that would draw on your areas of greatest strength or seek to improve your knowledge and skills in weaker subject areas. However, if your grades and scores differ significantly, talk with your counselor about possible reasons for the differences.

Comparing Your Scores to Those of Enrolled First-Year College Students

Another way to understand your ACT test scores and ranks is by comparing them to those of students enrolled at colleges or universities you're interested in attending. This information can be very useful as you make decisions about applying for college. Keep in mind that admissions offices use a number of measures—including high school grades, recommendations, and extracurricular activities—to determine how students are likely to perform at their schools. Still, knowing that your ACT test scores are similar to those of students already enrolled at a college or university you're considering may make you more confident in applying for admission there.

Using ACT College and Career Readiness Standards to Help You Understand Your ACT Scores

After you calculate your scores, you may wonder what your test scores mean regarding how well you are prepared to tackle college-level courses. In other words, what do your test scores tell you about your knowledge and skills in English, math, reading, and science? One way to understand this is to consider your scores from the perspective of what students who have that score are likely to know and be able to do. ACT developed the College and Career Readiness Standards to tell you exactly that.

What Are the ACT College and Career Readiness Standards?

The ACT College and Career Readiness Standards are sets of statements that describe what students are *likely* to know and be able to do in each content area based on their scores on each of the tests (English, mathematics, reading, science, and writing). The statements serve as score descriptors and reflect a progression of skills and knowledge in a particular content area. The College and Career Readiness Standards are reported in terms of score range, so that the statements describe the knowledge and skills that students *typically* demonstrate who score in these different ranges on the multiple-choice tests: 13–15, 16–19, 20–23, 24–27, 28–32, 33–36. A score of 1–12 indicates the student is most likely beginning to develop the knowledge and skills described in the 13–15 score range for that particular test. All the College and Career Readiness Standards are cumulative, meaning that students typically can also demonstrate the skills and knowledge described in the score ranges below the range in which they scored.

How Can the ACT College and Career Readiness Standards Help You?

The purpose of the ACT College and Career Readiness Standards is to help you and others better understand what your ACT scores indicate about the knowledge and skills you likely have and what areas might need further development for you to be better prepared for college.

Because the ACT College and Career Readiness Standards provide statements that describe what you are *likely* to know and be able to do, you can use that information to help zero in on what specific steps you should take to further develop your college readiness. If, for example, you scored in the 16–19 range on the English test, you might infer that you are likely able to do and know the skills and knowledge described in the 13–15 and in the 16–19 range. You might choose to take a closer look at the standards in the 20–23 and higher score ranges to see what courses to take, or what instruction you might need, to develop those particular areas in order to be better prepared for college. In other words, you can use the ACT College and Career Readiness Standards to help you select courses and instruction that will focus on preparing you for college.

ACT College Readiness Benchmarks

ACT has identified the minimum score needed on each ACT test to indicate a 50% chance of obtaining a B or higher or about a 75% chance of obtaining a C or higher in the corresponding first-year college course. Your score report will have a visual representation of where you scored compared to the ACT College Readiness Benchmark.

ACT Test	ACT Benchmark Score	College Course
English	18	English Composition
Mathematics	22	Algebra
Reading	22	Social Sciences/Humanities
Science	23	Biology

To increase your college readiness, consider taking additional rigorous course work before you enter college. When you meet with your academic advisor to plan your first-year college courses, select courses that are appropriate for your academic background and reflect your planned curriculum.

Planning Your Education and Career

The *ACT Student Report* includes a College and Career Planning section that helps you explore college majors and occupations, consider your options, and develop plans. The information in this section is all about you. Majors and occupations you may want to explore have been listed here, because they are related to the interests you expressed or occupations you said you were considering.

Seeking Additional Information and Guidance

Your *ACT Student Report* will provide additional information to help you understand your ACT test results and use them to make important decisions about college and to explore possible future careers.

As you approach decisions about college and careers, be sure to take advantage of all the assistance you can find. Talk to your parents, counselors, and teachers; visit your local library; and talk directly to personnel at colleges in which you're interested. The more you can find out about all the educational options available to you and the level of your academic skills and knowledge (using such information as your ACT test results), the better prepared you'll be to make informed college and career choices.

ACT College and Career Readiness Standards—English

These standards describe what students who score in specific score ranges on the English test are likely to know and be able to do.

- Students who score in the 1–12 range are most likely beginning to develop the knowledge and skills assessed in the other ranges.

- The ACT College Readiness Benchmark for English is 18. Students who achieve this score on the ACT English test have a 50% likelihood of achieving a B or better in a first-year English composition course at a typical college. The knowledge and skills highly likely to be demonstrated by students who meet the benchmark are shaded.

Production of Writing

Score Range	Production of Writing: Topic Development in Terms of Purpose and Focus (TOD)
13–15	TOD 201. Delete material because it is obviously irrelevant in terms of the topic of the essay
16–19	TOD 301. Delete material because it is obviously irrelevant in terms of the focus of the essay TOD 302. Identify the purpose of a word or phrase when the purpose is simple (e.g., identifying a person, defining a basic term, using common descriptive adjectives) TOD 303. Determine whether a simple essay has met a straightforward goal
20–23	TOD 401. Determine relevance of material in terms of the focus of the essay TOD 402. Identify the purpose of a word or phrase when the purpose is straightforward (e.g., describing a person, giving examples) TOD 403. Use a word, phrase, or sentence to accomplish a straightforward purpose (e.g., conveying a feeling or attitude)
24–27	TOD 501. Determine relevance of material in terms of the focus of the paragraph TOD 502. Identify the purpose of a word, phrase, or sentence when the purpose is fairly straightforward (e.g., identifying traits, giving reasons, explaining motivations) TOD 503. Determine whether an essay has met a specified goal TOD 504. Use a word, phrase, or sentence to accomplish a fairly straightforward purpose (e.g., sharpening an essay's focus, illustrating a given statement)

18

Score Range	Production of Writing: Topic Development in Terms of Purpose and Focus (TOD) (*continued*)
28–32	TOD 601. Determine relevance when considering material that is plausible but potentially irrelevant at a given point in the essay
	TOD 602. Identify the purpose of a word, phrase, or sentence when the purpose is subtle (e.g., supporting a later point, establishing tone) or when the best decision is to delete the text in question
	TOD 603. Use a word, phrase, or sentence to accomplish a subtle purpose (e.g., adding emphasis or supporting detail, expressing meaning through connotation)
33–36	TOD 701. Identify the purpose of a word, phrase, or sentence when the purpose is complex (e.g., anticipating a reader's need for background information) or requires a thorough understanding of the paragraph and essay
	TOD 702. Determine whether a complex essay has met a specified goal
	TOD 703. Use a word, phrase, or sentence to accomplish a complex purpose, often in terms of the focus of the essay

Score Range	Production of Writing: Organization, Unity, and Cohesion (ORG)
13–15	ORG 201. Determine the need for transition words or phrases to establish time relationships in simple narrative essays (e.g., *then*, *this time*)
16–19	ORG 301. Determine the most logical place for a sentence in a paragraph
	ORG 302. Provide a simple conclusion to a paragraph or essay (e.g., expressing one of the essay's main ideas)
20–23	ORG 401. Determine the need for transition words or phrases to establish straightforward logical relationships (e.g., *first*, *afterward*, *in response*)
	ORG 402. Determine the most logical place for a sentence in a straightforward essay
	ORG 403. Provide an introduction to a straightforward paragraph
	ORG 404. Provide a straightforward conclusion to a paragraph or essay (e.g., summarizing an essay's main idea or ideas)
	ORG 405. Rearrange the sentences in a straightforward paragraph for the sake of logic

18

(*continued*)

Score Range	Production of Writing: Organization, Unity, and Cohesion (ORG) (continued)
24–27	ORG 501. Determine the need for transition words or phrases to establish subtle logical relationships within and between sentences (e.g., *therefore*, *however*, *in addition*)
	ORG 502. Provide a fairly straightforward introduction or conclusion to or transition within a paragraph or essay (e.g., supporting or emphasizing an essay's main idea)
	ORG 503. Rearrange the sentences in a fairly straightforward paragraph for the sake of logic
	ORG 504. Determine the best place to divide a paragraph to meet a particular rhetorical goal
	ORG 505. Rearrange the paragraphs in an essay for the sake of logic
28–32	ORG 601. Determine the need for transition words or phrases to establish subtle logical relationships within and between paragraphs
	ORG 602. Determine the most logical place for a sentence in a fairly complex essay
	ORG 603. Provide a subtle introduction or conclusion to or transition within a paragraph or essay (e.g., echoing an essay's theme or restating the main argument)
	ORG 604. Rearrange the sentences in a fairly complex paragraph for the sake of logic and coherence
33–36	ORG 701. Determine the need for transition words or phrases, basing decisions on a thorough understanding of the paragraph and essay
	ORG 702. Provide a sophisticated introduction or conclusion to or transition within a paragraph or essay, basing decisions on a thorough understanding of the paragraph and essay (e.g., linking the conclusion to one of the essay's main images)

Score Range	Production of Writing: Knowledge of Language (KLA)
13–15	KLA 201. Revise vague, clumsy, and confusing writing that creates obvious logic problems
16–19	KLA 301. Delete obviously redundant and wordy material
	KLA 302. Revise expressions that deviate markedly from the style and tone of the essay
20–23	KLA 401. Delete redundant and wordy material when the problem is contained within a single phrase (e.g., "alarmingly startled," "started by reaching the point of beginning")
	KLA 402. Revise expressions that deviate from the style and tone of the essay
	KLA 403. Determine the need for conjunctions to create straightforward logical links between clauses
	KLA 404. Use the word or phrase most appropriate in terms of the content of the sentence when the vocabulary is relatively common
24–27	KLA 501. Revise vague, clumsy, and confusing writing
	KLA 502. Delete redundant and wordy material when the meaning of the entire sentence must be considered
	KLA 503. Revise expressions that deviate in subtle ways from the style and tone of the essay
	KLA 504. Determine the need for conjunctions to create logical links between clauses
	KLA 505. Use the word or phrase most appropriate in terms of the content of the sentence when the vocabulary is uncommon
28–32	KLA 601. Revise vague, clumsy, and confusing writing involving sophisticated language
	KLA 602. Delete redundant and wordy material that involves fairly sophisticated language (e.g., "the outlook of an aesthetic viewpoint") or that sounds acceptable as conversational English
	KLA 603. Determine the need for conjunctions to create subtle logical links between clauses
	KLA 604. Use the word or phrase most appropriate in terms of the content of the sentence when the vocabulary is fairly sophisticated
33–36	KLA 701. Delete redundant and wordy material that involves sophisticated language or complex concepts or where the material is redundant in terms of the paragraph or essay as a whole
	KLA 702. Use the word or phrase most appropriate in terms of the content of the sentence when the vocabulary is sophisticated

18

Score Range	Conventions of Standard English Sentence Structure and Formation (SST)
13–15	SST 201. Determine the need for punctuation or conjunctions to join simple clauses SST 202. Recognize and correct inappropriate shifts in verb tense between simple clauses in a sentence or between simple adjoining sentences
16–19	SST 301. Determine the need for punctuation or conjunctions to correct awkward-sounding fragments and fused sentences as well as obviously faulty subordination and coordination of clauses SST 302. Recognize and correct inappropriate shifts in verb tense and voice when the meaning of the entire sentence must be considered
20–23	SST 401. Recognize and correct marked disturbances in sentence structure (e.g., faulty placement of adjectives, participial phrase fragments, missing or incorrect relative pronouns, dangling or misplaced modifiers, lack of parallelism within a simple series of verbs)
24–27	SST 501. Recognize and correct disturbances in sentence structure (e.g., faulty placement of phrases, faulty coordination and subordination of clauses, lack of parallelism within a simple series of phrases) SST 502. Maintain consistent and logical verb tense and pronoun person on the basis of the preceding clause or sentence
28–32	SST 601. Recognize and correct subtle disturbances in sentence structure (e.g., danglers where the intended meaning is clear but the sentence is ungrammatical, faulty subordination and coordination of clauses in long or involved sentences) SST 602. Maintain consistent and logical verb tense and voice and pronoun person on the basis of the paragraph or essay as a whole
33–36	SST 701. Recognize and correct very subtle disturbances in sentence structure (e.g., weak conjunctions between independent clauses, run-ons that would be acceptable in conversational English, lack of parallelism within a complex series of phrases or clauses)

18

Score Range	Conventions of Standard English Usage Conventions (USG)
13–15	USG 201. Form the past tense and past participle of irregular but commonly used verbs
	USG 202. Form comparative and superlative adjectives
16–19	USG 301. Determine whether an adjective form or an adverb form is called for in a given situation
	USG 302. Ensure straightforward subject-verb agreement
	USG 303. Ensure straightforward pronoun-antecedent agreement
	USG 304. Use idiomatically appropriate prepositions in simple contexts
	USG 305. Use the appropriate word in frequently confused pairs (e.g., *there* and *their*, *past* and *passed*, *led* and *lead*)
20–23	USG 401. Use the correct comparative or superlative adjective or adverb form depending on context (e.g., "He is the oldest of my three brothers")
	USG 402. Ensure subject-verb agreement when there is some text between the subject and verb
	USG 403. Use idiomatically appropriate prepositions, especially in combination with verbs (e.g., *long for*, *appeal to*)
	USG 404. Recognize and correct expressions that deviate from idiomatic English
24–27	USG 501. Form simple and compound verb tenses, both regular and irregular, including forming verbs by using *have* rather than *of* (e.g., "would have gone," not "would of gone")
	USG 502. Ensure pronoun-antecedent agreement when the pronoun and antecedent occur in separate clauses or sentences
	USG 503. Recognize and correct vague and ambiguous pronouns
28–32	USG 601. Ensure subject-verb agreement in some challenging situations (e.g., when the subject-verb order is inverted or when the subject is an indefinite pronoun)
	USG 602. Correctly use reflexive pronouns, the possessive pronouns *its* and *your*, and the relative pronouns *who* and *whom*
	USG 603. Use the appropriate word in less-common confused pairs (e.g., *allude* and *elude*)
33–36	USG 701. Ensure subject-verb agreement when a phrase or clause between the subject and verb suggests a different number for the verb
	USG 702. Use idiomatically and contextually appropriate prepositions in combination with verbs in situations involving sophisticated language or complex concepts

18

Score Range	Conventions of Standard English Conventions (PUN)
13–15	PUN 201. Delete commas that create basic sense problems (e.g., between verb and direct object)
16–19	PUN 301. Delete commas that markedly disturb sentence flow (e.g., between modifier and modified element)
	PUN 302. Use appropriate punctuation in straightforward situations (e.g., simple items in a series)
20–23	PUN 401. Delete commas when an incorrect understanding of the sentence suggests a pause that should be punctuated (e.g., between verb and direct object clause)
	PUN 402. Delete apostrophes used incorrectly to form plural nouns
	PUN 403. Use commas to avoid obvious ambiguity (e.g., to set off a long introductory element from the rest of the sentence when a misreading is possible)
	PUN 404. Use commas to set off simple parenthetical elements
24–27	PUN 501. Delete commas in long or involved sentences when an incorrect understanding of the sentence suggests a pause that should be punctuated (e.g., between the elements of a compound subject or compound verb joined by *and*)
	PUN 502. Recognize and correct inappropriate uses of colons and semicolons
	PUN 503. Use punctuation to set off complex parenthetical elements
	PUN 504. Use apostrophes to form simple possessive nouns
28–32	PUN 601. Use commas to avoid ambiguity when the syntax or language is sophisticated (e.g., to set off a complex series of items)
	PUN 602. Use punctuation to set off a nonessential/nonrestrictive appositive or clause
	PUN 603. Use apostrophes to form possessives, including irregular plural nouns
	PUN 604. Use a semicolon to link closely related independent clauses
33–36	PUN 701. Delete punctuation around essential/restrictive appositives or clauses
	PUN 702. Use a colon to introduce an example or an elaboration

18

ACT College and Career Readiness Standards—Mathematics

These standards describe what students who score in specific score ranges on the math test are likely to know and be able to do. For more information about the ACT College and Career Readiness Standards in mathematics, go to www.act.org/standard/planact/math/mathnotes.html.

- Students who score in the 1–12 range are most likely beginning to develop the knowledge and skills assessed in the other ranges.

- The ACT College Readiness Benchmark for mathematics is 22. Students who achieve this score on the ACT mathematics test have a 50% likelihood of achieving a B or better in a first-year college algebra course at a typical college. The knowledge and skills highly likely to be demonstrated by students who meet the benchmark are shaded.

Score Range	Number and Quantity (N)
13–15	N 201. Perform one-operation computation with whole numbers and decimals N 202. Recognize equivalent fractions and fractions in lowest terms N 203. Locate positive rational numbers (expressed as whole numbers, fractions, decimals, and mixed numbers) on the number line
16–19	N 301. Recognize one-digit factors of a number N 302. Identify a digit's place value N 303. Locate rational numbers on the number line Note: A matrix as a representation of data is treated here as a basic table.
20–23	N 401. Exhibit knowledge of elementary number concepts such as rounding, the ordering of decimals, pattern identification, primes, and greatest common factor N 402. Write positive powers of 10 by using exponents N 403. Comprehend the concept of length on the number line, and find the distance between two points N 404. Understand absolute value in terms of distance N 405. Find the distance in the coordinate plane between two points with the same x-coordinate or y-coordinate N 406. Add two matrices that have whole number entries
24–27	N 501. Order fractions N 502. Find and use the least common multiple N 503. Work with numerical factors N 504. Exhibit some knowledge of the complex numbers N 505. Add and subtract matrices that have integer entries

22

(continued)

Score Range	Number and Quantity (N) (*continued*)
28–32	N 601. Apply number properties involving prime factorization
	N 602. Apply number properties involving even/odd numbers and factors/multiples
	N 603. Apply number properties involving positive/negative numbers
	N 604. Apply the facts that π is irrational and that the square root of an integer is rational only if that integer is a perfect square
	N 605. Apply properties of rational exponents
	N 606. Multiply two complex numbers
	N 607. Use relations involving addition, subtraction, and scalar multiplication of vectors and of matrices
33–36	N 701. Analyze and draw conclusions based on number concepts
	N 702. Apply properties of rational numbers and the rational number system
	N 703. Apply properties of real numbers and the real number system, including properties of irrational numbers
	N 704. Apply properties of complex numbers and the complex number system
	N 705. Multiply matrices
	N 706. Apply properties of matrices and properties of matrices as a number system

Because algebra and functions are closely connected, some standards apply to both categories.

Score Range	Algebra (A)	Functions (F)
13–15	AF 201. Solve problems in one or two steps using whole numbers and using decimals in the context of money	
	A 201. Exhibit knowledge of basic expressions (e.g., identify an expression for a total as $b + g$) A 202. Solve equations in the form $x + a = b$, where a and b are whole numbers or decimals	F 201. Extend a given pattern by a few terms for patterns that have a constant increase or decrease between terms
16–19	AF 301. Solve routine one-step arithmetic problems using positive rational numbers, such as single-step percent	
	AF 302. Solve some routine two-step arithmetic problems	
	AF 303. Relate a graph to a situation described qualitatively in terms of familiar properties such as before and after, increasing and decreasing, higher and lower	
	AF 304. Apply a definition of an operation for whole numbers (e.g., $a \bullet b = 3a - b$)	

Score Range	Algebra (A)	Functions (F)
	A 301. Substitute whole numbers for unknown quantities to evaluate expressions A 302. Solve one-step equations to get integer or decimal answers A 303. Combine like terms (e.g., $2x + 5x$)	F 301. Extend a given pattern by a few terms for patterns that have a constant factor between terms
20–23	AF 401. Solve routine two-step or three-step arithmetic problems involving concepts such as rate and proportion, tax added, percentage off, and estimating by using a given average value in place of actual values AF 402. Perform straightforward word-to-symbol translations AF 403. Relate a graph to a situation described in terms of a starting value and an additional amount per unit (e.g., unit cost, weekly growth)	
	A 401. Evaluate algebraic expressions by substituting integers for unknown quantities A 402. Add and subtract simple algebraic expressions A 403. Solve routine first-degree equations A 404. Multiply two binomials A 405. Match simple inequalities with their graphs on the number line (e.g., $x > -3$) A 406. Exhibit knowledge of slope	F 401. Evaluate linear and quadratic functions, expressed in function notation, at integer values
24–27	AF 501. Solve multistep arithmetic problems that involve planning or converting common derived units of measure (e.g., feet per second to miles per hour) AF 502. Build functions and write expressions, equations, or inequalities with a single variable for common pre-algebra settings (e.g., rate and distance problems and problems that can be solved by using proportions) AF 503. Match linear equations with their graphs in the coordinate plane	

22

(continued)

(continued)

Score Range	Algebra (A)	Functions (F)
	A 501. Recognize that when numerical quantities are reported in real-world contexts, the numbers are often rounded	F 501. Evaluate polynomial functions, expressed in function notation, at integer values
	A 502. Solve real-world problems by using first-degree equations	F 502. Find the next term in a sequence described recursively
	A 503. Solve first-degree inequalities when the method does not involve reversing the inequality sign	F 503. Build functions and use quantitative information to identify graphs for relations that are proportional or linear
	A 504. Match compound inequalities with their graphs on the number line (e.g., $-10.5 < x < 20.3$)	F 504. Attend to the difference between a function modeling a situation and the reality of the situation
	A 505. Add, subtract, and multiply polynomials	F 505. Understand the concept of a function as having a well-defined output value at each valid input value
	A 506. Identify solutions to simple quadratic equations	F 506. Understand the concept of domain and range in terms of valid input and output, and in terms of function graphs
	A 507. Solve quadratic equations in the form $(x + a)(x + b) = 0$, where a and b are numbers or variables	
	A 508. Factor simple quadratics (e.g., the difference of squares and perfect square trinomials)	F 507. Interpret statements that use function notation in terms of their context
	A 509. Work with squares and square roots of numbers	F 508. Find the domain of polynomial functions and rational functions
	A 510. Work with cubes and cube roots of numbers	F 509. Find the range of polynomial functions
	A 511. Work with scientific notation	F 510. Find where a rational function's graph has a vertical asymptote
	A 512. Work problems involving positive integer exponents	F 511. Use function notation for simple functions of two variables
	A 513. Determine when an expression is undefined	
	A 514. Determine the slope of a line from an equation	

Score Range	Algebra (A)	Functions (F)
28–32	AF 601. Solve word problems containing several rates, proportions, or percentages AF 602. Build functions and write expressions, equations, and inequalities for common algebra settings (e.g., distance to a point on a curve and profit for variable cost and demand) AF 603. Interpret and use information from graphs in the coordinate plane AF 604. Given an equation or function, find an equation or function whose graph is a translation by a specified amount up or down	
	A 601. Manipulate expressions and equations A 602. Solve linear inequalities when the method involves reversing the inequality sign A 603. Match linear inequalities with their graphs on the number line A 604. Solve systems of two linear equations A 605. Solve quadratic equations A 606. Solve absolute value equations	F 601. Relate a graph to a situation described qualitatively in terms of faster change or slower change F 602. Build functions for relations that are inversely proportional F 603. Find a recursive expression for the general term in a sequence described recursively F 604. Evaluate composite functions at integer values
33–36	AF 701. Solve complex arithmetic problems involving percent of increase or decrease or requiring integration of several concepts (e.g., using several ratios, comparing percentages, or comparing averages) AF 702. Build functions and write expressions, equations, and inequalities when the process requires planning and/or strategic manipulation AF 703. Analyze and draw conclusions based on properties of algebra and/or functions AF 704. Analyze and draw conclusions based on information from graphs in the coordinate plane AF 705. Identify characteristics of graphs based on a set of conditions or on a general equation such as $y = ax^2 + c$ AF 706. Given an equation or function, find an equation or function whose graph is a translation by specified amounts in the horizontal and vertical directions	

(continued)

(continued)

Score Range	Algebra (A)	Functions (F)
	A 701. Solve simple absolute value inequalities A 702. Match simple quadratic inequalities with their graphs on the number line A 703. Apply the remainder theorem for polynomials, that $P(a)$ is the remainder when $P(x)$ is divided by $(x - a)$	F 701. Compare actual values and the values of a modeling function to judge model fit and compare models F 702. Build functions for relations that are exponential F 703. Exhibit knowledge of geometric sequences F 704. Exhibit knowledge of unit circle trigonometry F 705. Match graphs of basic trigonometric functions with their equations F 706. Use trigonometric concepts and basic identities to solve problems F 707. Exhibit knowledge of logarithms F 708. Write an expression for the composite of two simple functions

Score Range	Geometry (G)
13–15	G 201. Estimate the length of a line segment based on other lengths in a geometric figure G 202. Calculate the length of a line segment based on the lengths of other line segments that go in the same direction (e.g., overlapping line segments and parallel sides of polygons with only right angles) G 203. Perform common conversions of money and of length, weight, mass, and time within a measurement system (e.g., dollars to dimes, inches to feet, and hours to minutes)
16–19	G 301. Exhibit some knowledge of the angles associated with parallel lines G 302. Compute the perimeter of polygons when all side lengths are given G 303. Compute the area of rectangles when whole number dimensions are given G 304. Locate points in the first quadrant

Score Range	Geometry (G) (continued)
20–23	G 401. Use properties of parallel lines to find the measure of an angle
	G 402. Exhibit knowledge of basic angle properties and special sums of angle measures (e.g., 90°, 180°, and 360°)
	G 403. Compute the area and perimeter of triangles and rectangles in simple problems
	G 404. Find the length of the hypotenuse of a right triangle when only very simple computation is involved (e.g., 3–4–5 and 6–8–10 triangles)
	G 405. Use geometric formulas when all necessary information is given
	G 406. Locate points in the coordinate plane
	G 407. Translate points up, down, left, and right in the coordinate plane
24–27	G 501. Use several angle properties to find an unknown angle measure
	G 502. Count the number of lines of symmetry of a geometric figure
	G 503. Use symmetry of isosceles triangles to find unknown side lengths or angle measures
	G 504. Recognize that real-world measurements are typically imprecise and that an appropriate level of precision is related to the measuring device and procedure
	G 505. Compute the perimeter of simple composite geometric figures with unknown side lengths
	G 506. Compute the area of triangles and rectangles when one or more additional simple steps are required
	G 507. Compute the area and circumference of circles after identifying necessary information
	G 508. Given the length of two sides of a right triangle, find the third when the lengths are Pythagorean triples
	G 509. Express the sine, cosine, and tangent of an angle in a right triangle as a ratio of given side lengths
	G 510. Determine the slope of a line from points or a graph
	G 511. Find the midpoint of a line segment
	G 512. Find the coordinates of a point rotated 180° around a given center point

22

(continued)

Score Range	Geometry (G) (*continued*)
28–32	G 601. Use relationships involving area, perimeter, and volume of geometric figures to compute another measure (e.g., surface area for a cube of a given volume and simple geometric probability)
	G 602. Use the Pythagorean theorem
	G 603. Apply properties of 30°–60°–90°, 45°–45°–90°, similar, and congruent triangles
	G 604. Apply basic trigonometric ratios to solve right-triangle problems
	G 605. Use the distance formula
	G 606. Use properties of parallel and perpendicular lines to determine an equation of a line or coordinates of a point
	G 607. Find the coordinates of a point reflected across a vertical or horizontal line or across $y = x$
	G 608. Find the coordinates of a point rotated 90° about the origin
	G 609. Recognize special characteristics of parabolas and circles (e.g., the vertex of a parabola and the center or radius of a circle)
33–36	G 701. Use relationships among angles, arcs, and distances in a circle
	G 702. Compute the area of composite geometric figures when planning and/or visualization is required
	G 703. Use scale factors to determine the magnitude of a size change
	G 704. Analyze and draw conclusions based on a set of conditions
	G 705. Solve multistep geometry problems that involve integrating concepts, planning, and/or visualization

Score Range	Statistics and Probability (S)
13–15	S 201. Calculate the average of a list of positive whole numbers
	S 202. Extract one relevant number from a basic table or chart, and use it in a single computation
16–19	S 301. Calculate the average of a list of numbers
	S 302. Calculate the average given the number of data values and the sum of the data values
	S 303. Read basic tables and charts
	S 304. Extract relevant data from a basic table or chart and use the data in a computation
	S 305. Use the relationship between the probability of an event and the probability of its complement

Score Range	Statistics and Probability (S) (*continued*)
20–23	S 401. Calculate the missing data value given the average and all data values but one
	S 402. Translate from one representation of data to another (e.g., a bar graph to a circle graph)
	S 403. Determine the probability of a simple event
	S 404. Describe events as combinations of other events (e.g., using *and*, *or*, and *not*)
	S 405. Exhibit knowledge of simple counting techniques
24–27	S 501. Calculate the average given the frequency counts of all the data values
	S 502. Manipulate data from tables and charts
	S 503. Compute straightforward probabilities for common situations
	S 504. Use Venn diagrams in counting
	S 505. Recognize that when data summaries are reported in the real world, results are often rounded and must be interpreted as having appropriate precision
	S 506. Recognize that when a statistical model is used, model values typically differ from actual values
28–32	S 601. Calculate or use a weighted average
	S 602. Interpret and use information from tables and charts, including two-way frequency tables
	S 603. Apply counting techniques
	S 604. Compute a probability when the event and/or sample space are not given or obvious
	S 605. Recognize the concepts of conditional and joint probability expressed in real-world contexts
	S 606. Recognize the concept of independence expressed in real-world contexts
33–36	S 701. Distinguish among mean, median, and mode for a list of numbers
	S 702. Analyze and draw conclusions based on information from tables and charts, including two-way frequency tables
	S 703. Understand the role of randomization in surveys, experiments, and observational studies
	S 704. Exhibit knowledge of conditional and joint probability
	S 705. Recognize that part of the power of statistical modeling comes from looking at regularity in the differences between actual values and model values

22

ACT College and Career Readiness Standards—Reading

These standards describe what students who score in specific score ranges on the reading test are likely to know and be able to do.

- Students who score in the 1–12 range are most likely beginning to develop the knowledge and skills assessed in the other ranges.

- The ACT College Readiness Benchmark for reading is 22. Students who achieve this score on the ACT reading test have a 50% likelihood of achieving a B or better in a first-year social science course at a typical college. The knowledge and skills highly likely to be demonstrated by students who meet the benchmark are shaded.

Score Range	Close Reading (CLR)
13–15	CLR 201. Locate basic facts (e.g., names, dates, events) clearly stated in a passage CLR 202. Draw simple logical conclusions about the main characters in somewhat challenging literary narratives
16–19	CLR 301. Locate simple details at the sentence and paragraph level in somewhat challenging passages CLR 302. Draw simple logical conclusions in somewhat challenging passages
20–23	CLR 401. Locate important details in somewhat challenging passages CLR 402. Draw logical conclusions in somewhat challenging passages CLR 403. Draw simple logical conclusions in more challenging passages CLR 404. Paraphrase some statements as they are used in somewhat challenging passages
24–27	CLR 501. Locate and interpret minor or subtly stated details in somewhat challenging passages CLR 502. Locate important details in more challenging passages CLR 503. Draw subtle logical conclusions in somewhat challenging passages CLR 504. Draw logical conclusions in more challenging passages CLR 505. Paraphrase virtually any statement as it is used in somewhat challenging passages CLR 506. Paraphrase some statements as they are used in more challenging passages

22

Score Range	Close Reading (CLR) (*continued*)
28–32	CLR 601. Locate and interpret minor or subtly stated details in more challenging passages
	CLR 602. Locate important details in complex passages
	CLR 603. Draw subtle logical conclusions in more challenging passages
	CLR 604. Draw simple logical conclusions in complex passages
	CLR 605. Paraphrase virtually any statement as it is used in more challenging passages
33–36	CLR 701. Locate and interpret minor or subtly stated details in complex passages
	CLR 702. Locate important details in highly complex passages
	CLR 703. Draw logical conclusions in complex passages
	CLR 704. Draw simple logical conclusions in highly complex passages
	CLR 705. Draw complex or subtle logical conclusions, often by synthesizing information from different portions of the passage
	CLR 706. Paraphrase statements as they are used in complex passages

Score Range	Central Ideas, Themes, and Summaries (IDT)
13–15	IDT 201. Identify the topic of passages and distinguish the topic from the central idea or theme
16–19	IDT 301. Identify a clear central idea in straightforward paragraphs in somewhat challenging literary narratives
20–23	IDT 401. Infer a central idea in straightforward paragraphs in somewhat challenging literary narratives
	IDT 402. Identify a clear central idea or theme in somewhat challenging passages or their paragraphs
	IDT 403. Summarize key supporting ideas and details in somewhat challenging passages
24–27	IDT 501. Infer a central idea or theme in somewhat challenging passages or their paragraphs
	IDT 502. Identify a clear central idea or theme in more challenging passages or their paragraphs
	IDT 503. Summarize key supporting ideas and details in more challenging passages

22

(continued)

Score Range	Central Ideas, Themes, and Summaries (IDT) (*continued*)
28–32	IDT 601. Infer a central idea or theme in more challenging passages or their paragraphs
	IDT 602. Summarize key supporting ideas and details in complex passages
33–36	IDT 701. Identify or infer a central idea or theme in complex passages or their paragraphs
	IDT 702. Summarize key supporting ideas and details in highly complex passages

Score Range	Relationships (REL)
13–15	REL 201. Determine when (e.g., *first, last, before, after*) an event occurs in somewhat challenging passages
	REL 202. Identify simple cause-effect relationships within a single sentence in a passage
16–19	REL 301. Identify clear comparative relationships between main characters in somewhat challenging literary narratives
	REL 302. Identify simple cause-effect relationships within a single paragraph in somewhat challenging literary narratives
20–23	REL 401. Order simple sequences of events in somewhat challenging literary narratives
	REL 402. Identify clear comparative relationships in somewhat challenging passages
	REL 403. Identify clear cause-effect relationships in somewhat challenging passages
24–27	REL 501. Order sequences of events in somewhat challenging passages
	REL 502. Understand implied or subtly stated comparative relationships in somewhat challenging passages
	REL 503. Identify clear comparative relationships in more challenging passages
	REL 504. Understand implied or subtly stated cause-effect relationships in somewhat challenging passages
	REL 505. Identify clear cause-effect relationships in more challenging passages

22

Score Range	Relationships (REL) *(continued)*
28–32	REL 601. Order sequences of events in more challenging passages
	REL 602. Understand implied or subtly stated comparative relationships in more challenging passages
	REL 603. Identify clear comparative relationships in complex passages
	REL 604. Understand implied or subtly stated cause-effect relationships in more challenging passages
	REL 605. Identify clear cause-effect relationships in complex passages
33–36	REL 701. Order sequences of events in complex passages
	REL 702. Understand implied or subtly stated comparative relationships in complex passages
	REL 703. Identify clear comparative relationships in highly complex passages
	REL 704. Understand implied or subtly stated cause-effect relationships in complex passages
	REL 705. Identify clear cause-effect relationships in highly complex passages

Score Range	Craft and Structure: Word Meanings and Word Choice (WME)
13–15	WME 201. Understand the implication of a familiar word or phrase and of simple descriptive language
16–19	WME 301. Analyze how the choice of a specific word or phrase shapes meaning or tone in somewhat challenging passages when the effect is simple
	WME 302. Interpret basic figurative language as it is used in a passage
20–23	WME 401. Analyze how the choice of a specific word or phrase shapes meaning or tone in somewhat challenging passages
	WME 402. Interpret most words and phrases as they are used in somewhat challenging passages, including determining technical, connotative, and figurative meanings

22

(continued)

Score Range	Craft and Structure: Word Meanings and Word Choice (WME) (*continued*)
24–27	WME 501. Analyze how the choice of a specific word or phrase shapes meaning or tone in somewhat challenging passages when the effect is subtle
	WME 502. Analyze how the choice of a specific word or phrase shapes meaning or tone in more challenging passages
	WME 503. Interpret virtually any word or phrase as it is used in somewhat challenging passages, including determining technical, connotative, and figurative meanings
	WME 504. Interpret most words and phrases as they are used in more challenging passages, including determining technical, connotative, and figurative meanings
28–32	WME 601. Analyze how the choice of a specific word or phrase shapes meaning or tone in complex passages
	WME 602. Interpret virtually any word or phrase as it is used in more challenging passages, including determining technical, connotative, and figurative meanings
	WME 603. Interpret words and phrases in a passage that makes consistent use of figurative, general academic, domain-specific, or otherwise difficult language
33–36	WME 701. Analyze how the choice of a specific word or phrase shapes meaning or tone in passages when the effect is subtle or complex
	WME 702. Interpret words and phrases as they are used in complex passages, including determining technical, connotative, and figurative meanings
	WME 703. Interpret words and phrases in a passage that makes extensive use of figurative, general academic, domain-specific, or otherwise difficult language

Score Range	Craft and Structure: Text Structure (TST)
13–15	TST 201. Analyze how one or more sentences in passages relate to the whole passage when the function is stated or clearly indicated
16–19	TST 301. Analyze how one or more sentences in somewhat challenging passages relate to the whole passage when the function is simple
	TST 302. Identify a clear function of straightforward paragraphs in somewhat challenging literary narratives

Score Range	Craft and Structure: Text Structure (TST) *(continued)*
20–23	TST 401. Analyze how one or more sentences in somewhat challenging passages relate to the whole passage TST 402. Infer the function of straightforward paragraphs in somewhat challenging literary narratives TST 403. Identify a clear function of paragraphs in somewhat challenging passages TST 404. Analyze the overall structure of somewhat challenging passages
24–27	TST 501. Analyze how one or more sentences in somewhat challenging passages relate to the whole passage when the function is subtle TST 502. Analyze how one or more sentences in more challenging passages relate to the whole passage TST 503. Infer the function of paragraphs in somewhat challenging passages TST 504. Identify a clear function of paragraphs in more challenging passages TST 505. Analyze the overall structure of more challenging passages
28–32	TST 601. Analyze how one or more sentences in complex passages relate to the whole passage TST 602. Infer the function of paragraphs in more challenging passages TST 603. Analyze the overall structure of complex passages
33–36	TST 701. Analyze how one or more sentences in passages relate to the whole passage when the function is subtle or complex TST 702. Identify or infer the function of paragraphs in complex passages TST 703. Analyze the overall structure of highly complex passages

22

Score Range	Craft and Structure: Purpose and Point of View (PPV)
13–15	PPV 201. Recognize a clear intent of an author or narrator in somewhat challenging literary narratives
16–19	PPV 301. Recognize a clear intent of an author or narrator in somewhat challenging passages
20–23	PPV 401. Identify a clear purpose of somewhat challenging passages and how that purpose shapes content and style PPV 402. Understand point of view in somewhat challenging passages

22

(continued)

Score Range	Craft and Structure: Purpose and Point of View (PPV) (*continued*)
24–27	PPV 501. Infer a purpose in somewhat challenging passages and how that purpose shapes content and style PPV 502. Identify a clear purpose of more challenging passages and how that purpose shapes content and style PPV 503. Understand point of view in more challenging passages
28–32	PPV 601. Infer a purpose in more challenging passages and how that purpose shapes content and style PPV 602. Understand point of view in complex passages
33–36	PPV 701. Identify or infer a purpose in complex passages and how that purpose shapes content and style PPV 702. Understand point of view in highly complex passages

Score Range	Integration of Knowledge and Ideas: Arguments (ARG)
13–15	ARG 201. Analyze how one or more sentences in passages offer reasons for or support a claim when the relationship is clearly indicated
16–19	ARG 301. Analyze how one or more sentences in somewhat challenging passages offer reasons for or support a claim when the relationship is simple
20–23	ARG 401. Analyze how one or more sentences in somewhat challenging passages offer reasons for or support a claim ARG 402. Identify a clear central claim in somewhat challenging passages
24–27	ARG 501. Analyze how one or more sentences in more challenging passages offer reasons for or support a claim ARG 502. Infer a central claim in somewhat challenging passages ARG 503. Identify a clear central claim in more challenging passages
28–32	ARG 601. Analyze how one or more sentences in complex passages offer reasons for or support a claim ARG 602. Infer a central claim in more challenging passages
33–36	ARG 701. Analyze how one or more sentences in passages offer reasons for or support a claim when the relationship is subtle or complex ARG 702. Identify or infer a central claim in complex passages ARG 703. Identify a clear central claim in highly complex passages

22

Score Range	Integration of Knowledge and Ideas: Multiple Texts (SYN)
13–15	SYN 201. Make simple comparisons between two passages
16–19	SYN 301. Make straightforward comparisons between two passages
20–23	SYN 401. Draw logical conclusions using information from two literary narratives
24–27	SYN 501. Draw logical conclusions using information from two informational texts
28–32	SYN 601. Draw logical conclusions using information from multiple portions of two literary narratives
33–36	SYN 701. Draw logical conclusions using information from multiple portions of two informational texts

22

Text Complexity Rubric—Reading

This rubric describes reading passages for ACT Aspire™ Grade 8, ACT Aspire Early High School, and the ACT.

Literary Narratives: Stories and Literary Nonfiction

	Somewhat Challenging Literary Narratives	More Challenging Literary Narratives	Complex Literary Narratives	Highly Complex Literary Narratives
Purpose/Levels of Meaning	• Have a largely straightforward purpose (chiefly literary nonfiction) • Contain literal and inferential levels of meaning (chiefly stories)	• Have a largely straightforward to somewhat complex purpose (chiefly literary nonfiction) • Contain literal, inferential, and interpretive levels of meaning (chiefly stories)	• Have a somewhat complex to complex purpose; apparent purpose may differ from real purpose (chiefly literary nonfiction) • Contain literal, inferential, and interpretive levels of meaning (chiefly stories)	• Have a complex purpose; apparent purpose may differ from real purpose (chiefly literary nonfiction) • Contain literal, inferential, and interpretive levels of meaning (chiefly stories)

(continued)

(continued)

	Somewhat Challenging Literary Narratives	More Challenging Literary Narratives	Complex Literary Narratives	Highly Complex Literary Narratives
Structure	• Use a mostly straightforward structure and a wide range of transitions (chiefly literary nonfiction) • Offer insights into people, situations, and events (e.g., motives) • May contain subplots, flashbacks, and flash-forwards (chiefly stories) • Explore largely straightforward conflicts that may be internal or external (chiefly stories) • May have multiple narrators, with switches clearly signaled; main characters exhibit growth and change (chiefly stories)	• Use a somewhat complex structure and a full range of transitions (chiefly literary nonfiction) • Offer deep insights into people, situations, and events (e.g., motives in conflict) • May contain numerous subplots, flashbacks, and flash-forwards as well as parallel and nonlinear plots; may lack clear resolution (chiefly stories) • Explore subtle conflicts that may be internal or external (chiefly stories) • May have multiple narrators; main characters are well rounded (chiefly stories)	• Use a complex structure (chiefly literary nonfiction) • Offer sophisticated and profound insights into people, situations, and events (e.g., philosophical commentary) • May contain numerous subplots, flashbacks, and flash-forwards as well as parallel and nonlinear plots; may lack clear resolution (chiefly stories) • Explore complex conflicts that are largely internal and lack an obvious or easy resolution (e.g., moral dilemmas) (chiefly stories) • May have multiple and/or unreliable narrator(s); main characters are well rounded (chiefly stories)	• Use a highly complex structure (chiefly literary nonfiction) • Offer sophisticated and profound insights into people, situations, and events (e.g., philosophical commentary) • Contain plots that are intricate, nonlinear, and/or difficult to discern; may lack resolution or may not be plot driven (chiefly stories) • Explore complex conflicts that are largely internal and lack an obvious or easy resolution (e.g., moral dilemmas) (chiefly stories) • May have multiple and/or unreliable narrator(s); main characters are well rounded (chiefly stories)

	Somewhat Challenging Literary Narratives	More Challenging Literary Narratives	Complex Literary Narratives	Highly Complex Literary Narratives
Language	• Use some uncommon words and phrases (e.g., general academic [tier 2] words, archaic words, dialect) • Use varied sentence structures significantly more or less formal than in everyday language • Use some somewhat challenging nonliteral and figurative language and literary devices (e.g., symbols, irony) • Observe language conventions (e.g., standard paragraph breaks) (chiefly stories)	• Use some uncommon words and phrases (e.g., general academic [tier 2] words, archaic words, dialect) • Use varied, often complex, and formal sentence structures, with texts from earlier time periods containing structures uncommon in more modern reading • Consistently use somewhat challenging nonliteral and figurative language and literary devices (e.g., symbols, irony) • Largely observe language conventions, with some unconventional elements possible (e.g., dialogue marked with dashes) (chiefly stories)	• Consistently use uncommon words and phrases (e.g., general academic [tier 2] words, archaic words, dialect) • Use varied, often complex, and formal sentence structures, with texts from earlier time periods containing structures uncommon in more modern reading • Consistently use challenging nonliteral and figurative language and literary devices (e.g., extended metaphors, satire, parody) • May use unconventional language structures (e.g., stream-of-consciousness)	• Extensively use uncommon words and phrases (e.g., general academic [tier 2] words, archaic words, dialect) • Use varied, often complex, and formal sentence structures, with texts from earlier time periods containing structures uncommon in more modern reading • Extensively use challenging nonliteral and figurative language and literary devices (e.g., extended metaphors, satire, parody) • Use unconventional language structures (e.g., stream-of-consciousness)

(*continued*)

(continued)

	Somewhat Challenging Literary Narratives	More Challenging Literary Narratives	Complex Literary Narratives	Highly Complex Literary Narratives
Abstractness (chiefly literary nonfiction)	• Depict some abstract ideas and concepts that may be important to understanding the text	• Depict several abstract ideas and concepts that are essential to understanding the text	• Depict numerous abstract ideas and concepts that are essential to understanding the text	• Depict numerous abstract ideas and concepts that are essential to understanding the text
Density (chiefly literary nonfiction)	• Have moderate information/ concept density	• Have moderately high information/ concept density	• Have high information/ concept density	• Have very high information/ concept density
Knowledge Demands: Textual Analysis, Life Experiences, Cultural and Literary Knowledge	• Assume readers can read on literal and inferential levels • Assume readers can handle somewhat challenging themes and subject matter with some maturity and objectivity • Assume readers can relate to experiences outside of their own • Call on cultural or literary knowledge to some extent	• Assume readers can read on literal, inferential, and interpretive levels • Assume readers can handle somewhat challenging themes and subject matter with some maturity and objectivity • Assume readers can relate to experiences distinctly different from their own	• Assume readers can read on literal, inferential, and interpretive levels • Assume readers can handle challenging themes and subject matter with maturity and objectivity • Assume readers can relate to experiences distinctly different from their own • Call on cultural or literary knowledge to some extent	• Assume readers can read on literal, inferential, and interpretive levels • Assume readers can handle complex themes and subject matter with maturity and objectivity • Assume readers can relate to experiences distinctly different from their own • Require cultural or literary knowledge for full comprehension

	Somewhat Challenging Literary Narratives	More Challenging Literary Narratives	Complex Literary Narratives	Highly Complex Literary Narratives
	• Have low intertextuality (i.e., make no/few or unimportant connections to other texts); drawing connections between texts at the level of theme may enhance understanding and appreciation	• Call on cultural or literary knowledge to some extent • Have moderate intertextuality (i.e., make some important connections to other texts); drawing connections between texts may enhance understanding and appreciation	• Have moderate intertextuality (i.e., make some important connections to other texts); drawing connections between texts may enhance understanding and appreciation	• Have high intertextuality (i.e., make many important connections to other texts); drawing connections between texts is essential for full understanding and appreciation

Informational Texts: Social Science, Humanities, and Natural Science

	Somewhat Challenging Informational Texts	More Challenging Informational Texts	Complex Informational Texts	Highly Complex Informational Texts
Purpose	• Have a largely straightforward purpose	• Have a largely straightforward to somewhat complex purpose	• Have a somewhat complex to complex purpose; apparent purpose may differ from real purpose	• Have a complex purpose; apparent purpose may differ from real purpose

(continued)

(continued)

	Somewhat Challenging Informational Texts	More Challenging Informational Texts	Complex Informational Texts	Highly Complex Informational Texts
Structure	• Use a mostly straightforward structure and a wide range of transitions • Exhibit norms and conventions of a general discipline (e.g., natural science)	• Use a somewhat complex structure and a full range of transitions • Exhibit norms and conventions of a general discipline (e.g., natural science	• Use a complex structure • Exhibit norms and conventions of a general discipline (e.g., natural science)	• Use a highly complex and possibly highly formalized structure (e.g., journal article) • Exhibit norms and conventions of a specific discipline (e.g., biology)
Language	• Use some general academic [tier 2] and domain-specific [tier 3] words and phrases • Use varied and some long and complicated sentence structures	• Consistently use general academic [tier 2] and domain-specific [tier 3] words and phrases • Use varied and often complex sentence structures, with consistent use of long and complicated structures	• Consistently use general academic [tier 2] and domain-specific [tier 3] words and phrases • Use varied and often complex sentence structures, with consistent use of long and complicated structures	• Extensively use general academic [tier 2] and domain-specific [tier 3] words and phrases • Use varied and often complex sentence structures, with consistent use of long and complicated structures
Abstractness	• Depict some abstract ideas and concepts that may be important to understanding the text	• Depict several abstract ideas and concepts that are essential to understanding the text	• Depict numerous abstract ideas and concepts that are essential to understanding the text	• Depict numerous abstract ideas and concepts that are essential to understanding the text
Density	• Have moderate information/concept density	• Have moderately high information/concept density	• Have high information/concept density	• Have very high information/concept density

	Somewhat Challenging Informational Texts	**More Challenging Informational Texts**	**Complex Informational Texts**	**Highly Complex Informational Texts**
Knowledge Demands: Textual Analysis, Life Experiences, Content and Discipline Knowledge	• Assume readers can read on literal and inferential levels • Assume readers can handle somewhat challenging subject matter, including perspectives, values, and ideas unlike their own, with some maturity and objectivity • Assume readers have everyday knowledge and some broad content knowledge, with texts at the high end of the range assuming some content knowledge • Have low intertextuality (i.e., make no/few or unimportant connections to other texts); drawing connections between texts at the level of general concept may enhance understanding	• Assume readers can read on literal, inferential, and evaluative levels • Assume readers can handle somewhat challenging subject matter, including perspectives, values, and ideas unlike their own, with some maturity and objectivity • Assume readers have some content knowledge, with texts at the high end of the range assuming some discipline-specific content knowledge • Have moderate intertextuality (i.e., make some important connections to other texts); drawing connections between texts may enhance understanding	• Assume readers can read on literal, inferential, and evaluative levels • Assume readers can handle challenging subject matter, including perspectives, values, and ideas in opposition to their own, with maturity and objectivity • Assume readers have some discipline-specific content knowledge • Have moderate intertextuality (i.e., make some important connections to other texts); drawing connections between texts may enhance understanding	• Assume readers can read on literal, inferential, and evaluative levels • Assume readers can handle complex subject matter, including perspectives, values, and ideas in opposition to their own, with maturity and objectivity • Assume readers have extensive discipline-specific content knowledge, often in specialized subjects or areas • Have high intertextuality (i.e., make many important connections to other texts); drawing connections between texts is essential for full understanding

ACT College and Career Readiness Standards—Science

These standards describe what students who score in specific score ranges on the science test are likely to know and be able to do.

- Students who score in the 1–12 range are most likely beginning to develop the knowledge and skills assessed in the other ranges.

- The ACT College Readiness Benchmark for science is 23. Students who achieve this score on the ACT science test have a 50% likelihood of achieving a B or better in a first-year biology course at a typical college. The knowledge and skills highly likely to be demonstrated by students who meet the benchmark are shaded.

Score Range	Interpretation of Data (IOD)
13–15	IOD 201. Select one piece of data from a simple data presentation (e.g., a simple food web diagram)
	IOD 202. Identify basic features of a table, graph, or diagram (e.g., units of measurement)
	IOD 203. Find basic information in text that describes a simple data presentation
16–19	IOD 301. Select two or more pieces of data from a simple data presentation
	IOD 302. Understand basic scientific terminology
	IOD 303. Find basic information in text that describes a complex data presentation
	IOD 304. Determine how the values of variables change as the value of another variable changes in a simple data presentation
20–23	IOD 401. Select data from a complex data presentation (e.g., a phase diagram)
	IOD 402. Compare or combine data from a simple data presentation (e.g., order or sum data from a table)
	IOD 403. Translate information into a table, graph, or diagram
	IOD 404. Perform a simple interpolation or simple extrapolation using data in a table or graph
24–27	IOD 501. Compare or combine data from two or more simple data presentations (e.g., categorize data from a table using a scale from another table)
	IOD 502. Compare or combine data from a complex data presentation
	IOD 503. Determine how the values of variables change as the value of another variable changes in a complex data presentation
	IOD 504. Determine and/or use a simple (e.g., linear) mathematical relationship that exists between data
	IOD 505. Analyze presented information when given new, simple information

23

Score Range	Interpretation of Data (IOD) (*continued*)
28–32	IOD 601. Compare or combine data from a simple data presentation with data from a complex data presentation
	IOD 602. Determine and/or use a complex (e.g., nonlinear) mathematical relationship that exists between data
	IOD 603. Perform a complex interpolation or complex extrapolation using data in a table or graph
33–36	IOD 701. Compare or combine data from two or more complex data presentations
	IOD 702. Analyze presented information when given new, complex information

Score Range	Scientific Investigation (SIN)
13–15	SIN 201. Find basic information in text that describes a simple experiment
	SIN 202. Understand the tools and functions of tools used in a simple experiment
16–19	SIN 301. Understand the methods used in a simple experiment
	SIN 302. Understand the tools and functions of tools used in a complex experiment
	SIN 303. Find basic information in text that describes a complex experiment
20–23	SIN 401. Understand a simple experimental design
	SIN 402. Understand the methods used in a complex experiment
	SIN 403. Identify a control in an experiment
	SIN 404. Identify similarities and differences between experiments
	SIN 405. Determine which experiments used a given tool, method, or aspect of design
24–27	SIN 501. Understand a complex experimental design
	SIN 502. Predict the results of an additional trial or measurement in an experiment
	SIN 503. Determine the experimental conditions that would produce specified results
28–32	SIN 601. Determine the hypothesis for an experiment
	SIN 602. Determine an alternate method for testing a hypothesis
33–36	SIN 701. Understand precision and accuracy issues
	SIN 702. Predict the effects of modifying the design or methods of an experiment
	SIN 703. Determine which additional trial or experiment could be performed to enhance or evaluate experimental results

23

Score Range	Evaluation of Models, Inferences, and Experimental Results (EMI)
13–15	EMI 201. Find basic information in a model (conceptual)
16–19	EMI 301. Identify implications in a model EMI 302. Determine which models present certain basic information
20–23	EMI 401. Determine which simple hypothesis, prediction, or conclusion is, or is not, consistent with a data presentation, model, or piece of information in text EMI 402. Identify key assumptions in a model EMI 403. Determine which models imply certain information EMI 404. Identify similarities and differences between models
24–27	EMI 501. Determine which simple hypothesis, prediction, or conclusion is, or is not, consistent with two or more data presentations, models, and/or pieces of information in text EMI 502. Determine whether presented information, or new information, supports or contradicts a simple hypothesis or conclusion, and why EMI 503. Identify the strengths and weaknesses of models EMI 504. Determine which models are supported or weakened by new information EMI 505. Determine which experimental results or models support or contradict a hypothesis, prediction, or conclusion
28–32	EMI 601. Determine which complex hypothesis, prediction, or conclusion is, or is not, consistent with a data presentation, model, or piece of information in text EMI 602. Determine whether presented information, or new information, supports or weakens a model, and why EMI 603. Use new information to make a prediction based on a model
33–36	EMI 701. Determine which complex hypothesis, prediction, or conclusion is, or is not, consistent with two or more data presentations, models, and/or pieces of information in text EMI 702. Determine whether presented information, or new information, supports or contradicts a complex hypothesis or conclusion, and why

23

ACT College and Career Readiness Standards for science are measured in rich and authentic contexts based on science content that students encounter in science courses. This content includes the following:

Life Science/Biology

- Animal behavior
- Animal development and growth
- Body systems
- Cell structure and processes
- Ecology

- Evolution
- Genetics
- Homeostasis
- Life cycles
- Molecular basis of heredity

- Origin of life
- Photosynthesis
- Plant development, growth, structure
- Populations
- Taxonomy

Physical Science/Chemistry, Physics

- Atomic structure
- Chemical bonding, equations, nomenclature, reactions
- Electrical circuits
- Elements, compounds, mixtures
- Force and motions

- Gravitation
- Heat and work
- Kinetic and potential energy
- Magnetism
- Momentum

- The periodic table
- Properties of solutions
- Sound and light
- States, classes, and properties of matter
- Waves

Earth and Space Science

- Earthquakes and volcanoes
- Earth's atmosphere
- Earth's resources
- Fossils and geological time
- Geochemical cycles

- Groundwater
- Lakes, rivers, oceans
- Mass movements
- Plate tectonics
- Rocks, minerals

- Solar system
- Stars, galaxies, and the universe
- Water cycle
- Weather and climate
- Weathering and erosion

NOTES

NOTES

NOTES

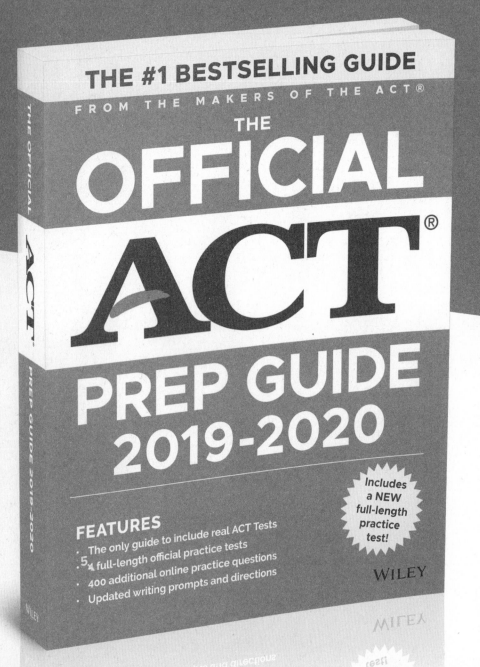